58 Years

MY LIFE IN MOUNTAIN RESCUE

MR. LYNN K. BUCHANAN

CreateSpace Independent Publishing Platform
North Charleston, South Carolina

TABLE OF CONTENTS

MEMORABILIA FROM FIFTY-EIGHT YEARS

Clockwise from the outside:

LKB Ski Patrol, climbing parka.
Retirement from Yakima Mtn. Rescue. Letter from YSO. He left out the first year—I was in Seattle MRC.
Yakima County IV Technician card.
Sheriff's Special Deputy Appointment – Sheriff John Thompson, 1970.
Ski Patrol National Avalanche Instructor name badge: #66.
1967 American Alpine Club membership pin.
Emergency Medical Technician card, 1972.
City of Yakima Mayor's pin.
CWMR service award, over 50 years.
CWMR Unit Membership card.
First Aid Instructors card. (WSC 1950).
Central WA Mtn. Rescue Operations Leader name badge.
Old REI membership: Number 3-704.

Center from top to bottom:

MRA Past Presidents pin.
1978 American Arctic Mountaineering Expedition shoulder patch.
Ski Patrol Avalanche Instructor card 1964.
Sheriff's Special Deputy Appointment – Sheriff Bert Guns, 1966.
Ski-Benders shoulder patch.

58 YEARS

This is to certify that

3-704 Dup.

L. K. BUCHANAN

is a member of

RECREATIONAL EQUIPMENT, Inc.
1525 11th Ave. • 523 Pike St.

Lloyd Anderson

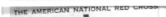

CENTRAL WASHINGTON MTN. RESCUE
LYNN BUCHANAN
OPERATIONS LEADER

Yakima County Health District

THIS CERTIFIES THAT

LYNN BUCHANAN

HAS SUCCESSFULLY COMPLETED THE REQUIRED
TRAINING PROGRAM FOR

PHYSICIANS TRAINED INTERVENOUS
and MEDICATION TECHNICIAN

AND IS HEREBY AUTHORIZED TO PERFORM THE DUTIES THEREOF
AS PRESCRIBED BY THE LAWS OF THE STATE OF WASHINGTON
AND LOCAL ORDINANCE.

GIVEN THIS 11th DAY OF January, 19 77

HEALTH OFFICER
This certification expires Jan. 11, 1978

THE AMERICAN NATIONAL RED CROSS

THIS CERTIFIES THAT

Lynn K. Buchanan

HAS COMPLETED THE INSTRUCTOR'S COURSE IN

First Aid

AT Pullman, Washington

Dorothes A. Coleman, Instructor

Dec. 14, 1950

County of Yakima,   I, JOHN H. THOMPSON,
Sheriff of Yakima County, State of Washington, reposing special confidence i
LYNN K. BUCHANAN

Yakima in said County and State, do hereby deputiz
appoint him as SPECIAL DEPUTY SHERIFF OF YAKIMA COUNTY, in the Stat
Washington, to perform the particular acts only as Special Deputy as are here
fter enumerated to be performed without pay, and revokable at my pleasure
the particular acts to be performed by said Special Deputy Sheriff shall be a
ows, to-wit: Unlimited

cial Deputy for the above purpose AND NONE OTHER WHATSOEVER.
ng distinctly understood that this appointment excludes said Special Deput
n exercising the power to levy any attachment or execution of any kind o
racter whatsoever, including the services of any Civil Process.
N WITNESS WHEREOF, I have hereunto set my hand this 25 da

March 19

The Central Washington Unit
MOUNTAIN RESCUE
ASSOCIATION

CERTIFIES THAT Lynn Buchanan THE
ABOVE UNIT IS A RESCUE MEMBER AND IS AUTHORIZED
TO USE THE APPROPRIATE MOUNTAIN RESCUE ASSOCIATION
INSIGNIA

1973

Pat Satghen, Unit Secretary

AVALANCHE
INSTRUCTOR

LYNN K. BUCHANAN

WHITE PASS SKI PATROL
LYNN BUCHANAN
NATIONAL AVALANCHE INSTRUCTOR

MOUNTAIN RESCUE
Lynn Buchanan
In Recognition Of
Over 30 Years
Of Service
Central Washington
Mountain Rescue

STATE OF WASHINGTON   CERTIFICATE OF APPOINTMENT
County of Yakima   I, BERT GUNS,
Sheriff of Yakima County, State of Washington, reposing special confidence in
LYNN K. BUCHANAN

of Yakima in said County and State, do hereby deputize
and appoint him as SPECIAL DEPUTY SHERIFF OF YAKIMA COUNTY,
in the State of Washington, to perform the particular acts only as Special Deputy
as are hereinafter enumerated to be performed without pay, and revokable at my
pleasure.
The particular acts to be performed by said Special Deputy Sheriff shall be as
follows: Unlimited

Special Deputy for the above purpose AND NONE OTHER WHATSOEVER.
It being distinctly understood that this appointment excludes said Special Deputy
from exercising the power to levy any attachment or execution of any kind of
character whatsoever, including the services of any Civil Process.
IN WITNESS WHEREOF, I have hereunto set my hand this 20 day
October 196 6

Sheriff of Yakima County, Washington

CITY OF YAKIMA
LYNN BUCHANAN
MAYOR

EMERGENCY
MEDICAL
TECHNICIAN

EMT

Lynn K. Buchanan

Howard Fanley   May 9, 1972

Wash. St. Dept. Social & Health Services   Date
Division of Health

Introduction

LYNN BUCHANAN'S FIFTY-EIGHT YEARS OF MOUNTAIN RESCUE HISTORY

THE FOLLOWING IS a bit of the history of my activities in Mountain Rescue, a history that covers fifty-eight years in the field as a volunteer, working with five consecutive elected sheriffs and two coroners in Yakima County, Washington; with Central Washington Mountain Rescue, as well as many missions with Seattle Mountain Rescue. There are many more stories, but this covers much of the variety. It tells the story of Central Washington Mountain Rescue (CWMR) from its start to modern times, from the days of landline telephone communication to modern radios. It covers missions from the days of long hikes into the mountains to reach the injured person to many modern helicopter missions.

In several of the stories that follow, you will see my mission statistics for that mission. However, I was just one member of the team of Mountain Rescue folks, so the total statistics for each mission are many multiples of the hours and miles I expended. Mountain Rescue missions are, above all, teamwork, and my stories are all told from the viewpoint of myself, one member of the TEAM that was accomplishing the rescue.

Most of these stories and pictures were a long time ago. If any readers have any names or corrections to add, send them to Lynn@lynnbuchanan.com.

I especially want to thank three ladies for spending an amazing amount of time proofreading, making suggestions, correcting my errors, and telling the computer and I to do it again! Thank you, Connie Buchanan, Grace Snodgrass and Sally Powers.

What started out as a short bit of reminiscing has turned into a tremendous amount of paper, ink, time, and research. Thanks to Don Rolfs for help with the printer and to members of Mountain Rescue for answers on questions: Mark Bales, Dave Rowland, Kathy Kessinger, Judy Hanna, Al Errington, Art Farash, Warren Thompson, Bill Davis and Fran Sharp, as well as Jim Linse for the use of his scrapbook. Also thanks to Dr. Jim Dodge and Dr. David Olson for reviewing the EMT and IV therapy parts. Thanks also to the folks at Dave Miller's EFCOM Communication for answering multiple questions about computers and printers. A special thanks is owed to Douglas Buchanan and David Buchanan, Spencer Hatton, Scott Sandsberry, and the *Yakima Herald-Republic* for permission to use their stories. There were many missions where, when I arrived back in Yakima, I stopped on my way back home and dropped off a roll of film for the *Herald* to use in their news story for the next day. In addition, I have added some stories from a couple of other members of Mountain Rescue: Lex Maxwell and Bob McCall. I asked for more, but Mountain Rescue folks are primarily mountain climbers, not writers. Thanks to all for their hours of volunteer time.

Let me add my thanks to the staff at Createspace for their help getting this finally printed.

– LYNN BUCHANAN, R-202 IN YAKIMA COUNTY, 2003

PUBLISHED ON FRIDAY, JANUARY 7, 1977
(YAKIMA HERALD-REPUBLIC)

Erring Rainier Climbers Rate More than $25 Fine

IF A LOGGING FIRM STARTS a forest fire, it almost certainly will be nailed for the thousands of dollars it costs to control the blaze. But when three mountain climbers, who failed to register for a winter climb, had to be plucked from Mt. Rainier's toughest route at a cost of many thousands of dollars, the National Park Service issued ticket citations carrying a $25 fine.

Where is the equity in that treatment?

If a miscue, even an entirely unintentional one, causes a commercial developer to damage any part of the environment, the super-activists among the environmentalists are quick to yell for heavy penalties. And often they may be justified. But where are the super-activists now, when three—perhaps of their own kind—are caught risking lives and costing bundles of taxpayers' cash to bring about their rescue from a foolish venture?

We invite a guest editorial from anyone among the many talented and often-summoned mountain rescue people in Yakima—whether agreeing with us or not that those three Mt. Rainier climbers should foot the bill for their own rescue.

In our opinion, a $25 ticket is an insult to the many hardy rescuers who risked life and limb to save those three from the consequences of their own mistakes.

❖ ❖ ❖

PUBLISHED ON JANUARY 13, 1977
(YAKIMA HERALD-REPUBLIC)

Rainier Rescuer Responds

EDITOR'S NOTE—The following guest editorial is by Lynn Buchanan, member of Central Washington Mountain Rescue, past president of National Mountain Rescue, and former member of the board of the American Alpine Club.

As one of those who "risked life and limb" on the search for the mountain climbers, I think someone has missed the point.

The climbers were fined because they failed to comply with a regulation. They did not register for their climb with the government official in charge of the paperwork. Quite probably there was no office open on the north side of Mt. Rainier when they went in. This would have required a drive to the park headquarters on the south side to register, then a drive back, losing a day's travel time and a day of good weather.

What else did the climbers do wrong except for failing to register so that the Park Service could add three more successful ascents to their mimeographed pages of annual statistics? They were qualified to climb. They made a successful ascent. They got caught in bad weather, and instead of trying to make a hazardous escape from the mountain, they used their heads and made a shelter to wait out the storm. When the weather improved, they descended the easiest route on the mountain, emerging from the clouds just above Schurman Hut to find all the "rescuers" looking for them. As I understand, they were a little unhappy that the search was started, since they had done the only safe and wise thing to do—wait out the worst of the weather.

Mountain climbing is one of the few activities left in which the individuals can match themselves against a known goal. Success or failure is not determined by what the rulebook says, how hard you hit the other guy, or whether the referee sees you step on the line. The individual's ability, stamina, skill, and equipment are pitted against altitude, distance, time, weather, and current conditions. The last two are variable and can change from hour to hour.

For many years, if a climber got into trouble, his success or failure to survive depended on how well he planned his trip. For serious situations, he could count on his friends (other climbers) to help when needed and wanted. This is still possible, but we are rapidly approaching the age of Big Brother. The agencies that control the climbing areas are taking more of the responsibility that formerly rested on the individual. They have their own rescue personnel. They must have their statistics. They complain of the cost. They get more appropriations. They need more statistics—and on around again.

There is a growing feeling in the climbing literature that the existence of "government" rescue service is leading to more dependence and less preplanning. If the agencies don't want to perform the rescue without pay, or gripe about the cost, they should get out of the rescue business. The climbers can take care of themselves. If a climber is hurt, there are other climbers, Mountain Rescue personnel, who can and will take care of the problem.

With the Mountain Rescue teams available, we can and will take care of the hunters, fishermen, hikers, pilots, etc. who need help. There were no complaints from the volunteers about the time or cost of the Rainier search. We were glad to have had a successful search. We are not above asking for help from the military, because we know that they only help when it does not interfere with their primary mission. If the agencies that complain of the cost of rescues would disband their paid personnel (and quit showing the volunteer as an expense), the "bundle of tax-payer cash" would diminish dramatically.

When you talk of "bundles of taxpayers' cash," I am reminded of a report at the last Washington Mountain Rescue Association meeting on costs of rescue in one National Park. A Park Service representative reported that rescues cost $36,000 last year; $19,000 of Park Service money and $17,000 of non-park expenses, plus military assistance. That was for 34 missions, four of which were for climbers.

After being asked for details, it was broken down as $19,000—mostly the time of rangers who were on salary. They would have been walking trails, doing paperwork, and talking to park visitors if they hadn't been participating in the rescues or searches. The $17,000 "cost" was based on man-hours expended by volunteers. The Department of Emergency Services has compiled a list of volunteer services with a price tag per hour to show what the service would cost if it was done by paid employees. Instead of being used to show the value of volunteer work, it is now being used by some agencies to show a cost figure, in this case a "cost" of $17,000.

Keep in mind that of their $36,000 cost, only $19,000 was actually taxpayers' money, and most of that was for vehicles and personnel already doing their assigned task—would have been paid whether or not there was a rescue. The balance, or $17,000, was purely hypothetical; no money was spent or received.

The third portion—military aid—is again a cost of the tax-payer that will go on regardless of rescues. Military pilots will fly a required number of hours per month, whether they fly on rescues or fly back and forth from the airport to the Firing Center. They must fly to maintain proficiency. They burn fuel and wear out engines (and occasionally bend helicopters) every day at every military installation, but there is no complaint because it is necessary for training. When the military gets a chance to assist on a rescue, they get some realistic training—flying to and from unprepared spots, as they would have to do in a conflict. It gives the taxpayer direct benefit for the taxes withheld from our paychecks.

I would like to point out that in this county we are fortunate to have a sheriff who has been on the trails carrying a pack on more than one rescue. Before he became sheriff, he accompanied the Mountain Rescue volunteers on several missions. With this background, he has organized the search and rescue volunteers to handle missions with a minimum of expense to the taxpayers. The sheriff's office coordinates and handles the paperwork while covering their primary duties—the volunteers do the fieldwork.

If the three climbers on Rainier had taken an extra half day and filled in the proper forms, they would not have been in violation—but the storm might have caught them in a place where they could not have made a shelter nor gotten off alive.

the wheel Buchanan retrieved from the wreckage. It showed the autopilot still on.

Of course, climbing up Mount Adams for rescue missions means you have to be in top shape. Don't worry about Buchanan. He's been going up steep inclines for 56 years, though he did admit last week's trek up to the crash site near Rimrock Lake was a bit much. It was a one-mile hike in, with a heart-thumping 3,000-foot elevation gain. Going up wasn't the problem, but coming down was, especially when you are hefting 40 pounds in your backpack.

While he leaves free climbing up vertical rock walls to others, he has helped injured climbers get down from them.

One such rescue happened on Kloochman Rock, a rugged outcropping of basalt near Rimrock. A climber had tried to summit the rock wall along the east side. He fell, and popped out every piton except the last one, which saved his life. Knocked unconscious by the fall, his limp body swayed as he dangled from his climbing rope 50 feet in the air. Buchanan soon arrived with a team of mountain rescue volunteers and rigged a pulley system to lower the injured climber to safety.

The next day Buchanan was there again with several other climbers to retrieve the man's ropes and equipment. Now you would think the injured climber would be grateful and would, at least once, have sent a card of thanks to Buchanan and his fellow mountain rescuers.

Nope.

But Buchanan doesn't seem bothered. He says often that the hiker or climber they rescue is embarrassed by the entire episode. They blame themselves for doing something stupid. And, of course, it ends up as a story in the newspaper, a public reminder of their act of personal stupidity.

But had there been survivors at last Sunday night's crash, I bet the families would have said thanks. We all would have. Volunteers like Buchanan and his wife Connie are rare, and getting rarer.

So the next time you see Lynn Buchanan, thank him. You will, no doubt, recognize him. He was on the Yakima City Council for more than two decades, and he's the guy riding his bike around town, in all types of weather.

So say thanks. It's obvious he hasn't gotten enough of those over the years. It's the least we can do for someone who stirs from a deep sleep in the early morning hours and honors an urgent plea: "We need your help."

This was a news article that appeared with a photo in the *Yakima Herald-Republic* on Sunday, 14 October 2007, after the Cessna Grand Caravan (C-208) was recovered with the remains of the 10 persons who had been aboard.

PUBLISHED ON THURSDAY, JANUARY 20, 2005
(YAKIMA HERALD-REPUBLIC)

From the Top
By Scott Sandsberry

FIFTEEN MINUTES.

For that amount of time, Andy Warhol once said, each of us would get to be famous. It's plenty of time—enough, even, for a life to begin or to end. For the tide to turn. For the weather to change. For battles to be won.

For heroes to be made.

Dave Mahre hasn't been famous—in the global sense—for even 15 minutes. Certainly not as famous as, say, his twin sons Phil and Steve, Olympic icons who are arguably the biggest names in American skiing history.

To be sure, Dave Mahre is well renowned and internationally respected among climbers. In the Pacific Northwest climbing community, in fact, the 78-year-old Yakima man will almost certainly remain a luminary long after he's gone.

He's had a full life, one in which he was married to the same woman for nearly five decades, raised nine children, was instrumental in the growth of the White Pass ski resort, climbed numerous mountains—many of them perilous first ascents—and made more friends than he can count.

But the essence of Dave Mahre's nearly eight decades on the planet might best be described by 15 minutes.

Because there was a distinct possibility he would not survive them.

And they were all about somebody he didn't even know.

Faith and trust

It was September, 1968. By that time, he had already established himself as one of the grittiest climbers in a state full of them.

He and the Prater brothers from Ellensburg, Gene and Bill, had virtually rewritten the climbing history of the central part of the state, putting up numerous first ascents on the sheer walls and precipitous ridges of the Stuart Range.

"He's one of the top guys who ever climbed, and just one of the finest people who could be," recalls Bill Prater. "He could do everything—the finest natural athlete I've been out (climbing) with."

And one of the most fearless. In 1963, Mahre had led a four-man team on the first ascent of Mount Rainier's Willis Wall. The 4,000-foot wall—topped by a 300-foot, menacingly overhanging ice cliff—was so fraught with avalanche danger that it was long considered unclimbable at best, an absolute deathtrap at worst.

That reputation has remained: According to Mount Rainier rangers, it's been at least 15 years since any climber has even attempted to ascend Willis Wall.

"Davey was a natural climber," says Lex Maxwell of Yakima, who also had quite the mountaineering reputation. "It was a joy to climb with him, because you knew he'd hold up his end of the rope."

And that faith and trust, for climbers, is paramount. "When you're roped together," Bill Prater says, "you're depending on that other guy for your life—and you always knew you could depend on him."

That's why, on one of the two Everest expeditions Mahre participated on in the early 1980s, he gave up his own chance at the summit to help an altitude-stricken teammate back to base camp.

It's why, if you ask Mahre about his proudest climbing achievements, he's apt to change the subject to one he considers more inherently valuable.

"I've hung my neck out to dry a lot further on rescues in my life," he'll say, "than I ever did as a climber."

That Mahre would risk his life for others—something he did numerous times, both on summit bids and mountain rescues—surprises no one who knows him.

"Of course, it can't be just about you. You always make sure everybody gets out safely," says Kathee Forman, one of his five daughters. "That's one thing I was always taught: God first, others second and I'm third. My dad never put it in those words, but that's what he was saying."

Lots of snow, little hope

And so it was that Dave Mahre was out there in 1968 with two other courageous mountain rescue men, Lynn Buchanan and Lex Maxwell, trudging through thigh-deep snow in blinding 70 mph winds.

Their goal in that virtual whiteout: to rescue two stranded hikers who, lying hypothermic in sleeping bags at the 7,400-foot level of Old Snowy Mountain, might already have frozen to death.

Five hikers from the Portland area had taken off from White Pass intending to negotiate a 43-mile hike along the rugged Cascade Crest Trail (now called the Pacific Crest Trail). People at White Pass—including Mahre, who was then in the first decade of his 30-plus years as the ski area's mountain manager—had warned the hikers against it.

"We told them it was not really safe to do this after Labor Day, because the first storm we get is generally about Labor Day," Mahre says. "They started across against the advice."

Two nights later, sometime after midnight, a hiker—an Alaska fisheries biologist on vacation—staggered into White Pass during a withering storm and woke up the condominium manager with harrowing news: Three exhausted, hypothermic hikers were in his tent at McCall Basin, 7 1/2 miles away. Two others were higher still, far above Elk Pass, tentless and in far worse shape. The biologist had found the three, done what he could for them and gone for help.

Buchanan, Mahre and Maxwell led the six-man rescue team up into the teeth of the storm. After the 7 1/2-mile trek to McCall Basin, they found the first three hikers, and half of the rescuers stayed to tend to them.

Mahre, Maxwell and Buchanan pushed on.

Ironically, when Mahre had stepped atop Mount Adams as a teenager, achieving his first summit, he had encountered Maxwell. It was Mahre's first meeting with the man he describes now as "like a surrogate father, like a dad to me. He's one of the guys who pulled me through life."

On that day atop Adams, all Maxwell gave him was a tongue-lashing.

"What are you doing up on the summit by yourself with no rope and no ice ax?" he demanded of the young Mahre. "You better come to a Cascadian meeting and learn something about this or else go to the library and read something about mountaineering!"

So Mahre did.

Now, two decades later, he and his mentor were taking turns breaking deep-snow trail in a whiteout, while Buchanan—carrying the heaviest pack, filled with first-aid gear—followed behind.

The weather was horrendous, the visibility minimal and their chances of finding the two missing hikers almost nil. Mahre found himself deal-making with God, saying *Lord, if you get us out of here, I'll never do this again.*

Hours into this freezing march, Mahre recalls, Maxwell said, "Davey, we're only going to go 15 minutes more or we're not going to make it back. We're going to be dead ourselves."

Fifteen minutes passed.

"We gotta go back," Maxwell said.

Mahre was so cold he was in tears—something that, in those days, was very rare.

Recalls Mahre, "I said, 'No, let's give it a few more minutes.'"
Measuring up

For Dave Mahre, the tears came later. They began, in fact, only months later.

As Mahre was clearing a new ski run at White Pass, a falling snag from the top of a tree—a large piece, perhaps 10 to 12 inches in diameter and about 35 feet long—smashed into his head.

The fact that he was wearing a hard hat mattered little. The tree fractured his skull, inflicted spinal damage that, even now, causes him hip and leg pain, and shattered his jaw. (The name of the ski run is, itself, an homage to Mahre: Jaw Breaker.)

Mahre had what he swears was an out-of-body experience—that feeling of seeing his body from a higher vantage point, seeing his co-worker racing down the mountain to get help and a truck in ways he couldn't possibly have seen from his smashed-up, blood-covered, prone perspective. "Most people poo-poo about this and say you're hallucinating," Mahre says, "but it happened."

And it changed Mahre.

"I was never emotional before that. I was just a crazy wild nut, that's all," he says. "That was just like getting religion in a hurry."

"I never really saw my dad cry before that," says Phil Mahre, one of Dave's four sons. "Now he cries saying grace at the dinner table. He's a very emotional person, yet he's a tough individual."

It took toughness to be the climber he was and, occasionally, still is. It took ego, too, something Dave Mahre readily admits. But when he talks about his climbing, it doesn't sound like bragging.

He sounds, rather, like a tough little welterweight fighter—which Mahre was as a teenager in the Merchant Marines—who never backed away from a challenge.

"Climbing to me is a battle with yourself, your own shortcomings," he says. "It's not a religion, but it's damn close to being spiritual. It's a search inside yourself, to see whether you measure up."

And in that 1968 whiteout, Mahre—like Lex Maxwell and Lynn Buchanan alongside—measured up.

Only moments after Mahre had said, "Let's give it a few more minutes," he saw a discoloration in the sea of white. As he stepped closer, he stepped on something blanketed by the snow.

It was an arm.

They quickly dug out the person it belonged to, a 60-year-old Portland businessman named Garnett Cannon who was very near death. Cannon's hiking companion—buried nearby in two feet of snow—had already died.

The rescue trio all but carried Cannon down to safety; he survived the ordeal. Through the entire rescue effort, Mahre was so cold, so frozen to the bone, that he wasn't sure he would survive. Says Mahre, "I've never felt that far down the ladder in my life."

Still, as he had on so many mountains, he had reached the top of that ladder.

A few years ago, a woman approached Mahre in the day lodge at White Pass and said, "I know you don't know me, but maybe you remember my father."

Her father, of course, was Garnett Cannon. And she wanted to thank one of the men who saved his life.

Because the man Dave Mahre had been searching for—the somebody for whom he and others had risked far more than those 15 minutes, the somebody he didn't even know—was, to someone else, the most important person in the world.

AVALANCHE

By Douglas Buchanan

Douglas (in red gaiters) walking up the glacier toward the avalanche area. This avalanche came from the face of the glacier that extends from the left side of the large "V" on the canyon wall to the highest part of the rock face in the center of the photo. The avalanche fell about 2,500 feet and went over three fourths of a mile across the glacier before continuing a mile and a half down glacier to the foreground. It consisted of thousands of tons of ice.

I WAS JUST OUTSIDE the door of the tent, bending over, picking up some small items to put in my pack. I heard something; it was not the loud crack, or whap, or roar or thunder of the usual ice avalanche, just something, something quiet, distant, and indistinct. I looked up, turning to the wall. It was too large to really see and distinguish all of it. It was a wide front; it was just breaking over the edge, the top of the rock wall. It was coming straight, and it did not conform to the channels of the usual avalanches. My first thought and words were, "Oh, shit!" I can't be absolutely sure of the words I used, but I think I said, "Hey Jim, here comes a biggie. I think we better run and hide behind this ice block."

I moved along side of the tent. I felt no real sense of urgency. The ice block was right there. The avalanche had a great distance to fall. It usually took quite a while. And I didn't really think it could get to us. At the rear of the tent, I stepped up the slope and looked back. Jim was out of the tent alongside of the front and heading for the ice block. I didn't see anything in back of him, nothing, I didn't consider it at the time, but it was all white, there was no black rock wall there. I moved a short distance to the edge of the ice block, where it met the slope coming up. As I stepped over the edge, something was around me. I had expected to turn around and look back. But it was there. I was down behind the block. Things were hitting me on the head and shoulders. I could feel my hard hat being hammered. I lifted my hands. I was being pushed down. I tried to move my legs, but they were being buried and being moved. I wanted to move them. Then I was on my stomach, face down. I felt that something very huge had knocked me down, but it was too fast. I felt a great pressure all around me. I thought, "I'm being buried now." I verbally thought, "I'm dead now. This is going to be a cold lonely death."

All this was in an instant. I don't remember noise. It was all violent fury, encompassing and all white. And as fast as it happened, it stopped. There was swirling ice dust and my arms were free. My arms were free, I thought that and wondered why. I was head downhill. My arms were moving and I felt as though I were in concrete. I tried to turn my shoulders but that hurt. I was being held up to my shoulders. There was a big chunk of ice pushing against my chest. I hit it with my fist, nothing moved. I thought, "If my hands are free I can get out." I yelled, "Hang on, Jim, I'll be there in a minute." I thought he might be stuck like me and need help.

Before me the whole glacier valley was swirling, blowing snow and ice dust that was beginning to settle. I noticed the wind was blowing. I wondered how long it would take me to get out. I tried to move. My feet, my legs, my body could not move. They were held by a force unlike any other experience! I kept thinking I had crampons on because they were my only association with anything so solid. I tried to push the snow and ice. My effort was pitiful. I sank into a feeling I would never get out. I thought of Jim, but I knew he was on the other side of the ice block and that seemed a world away. I said nothing. I began to push the snow away from around that chunk of ice. I took off my hard hat and tried to scrape but I didn't have enough movement to use it and it seemed like a futile tool. I don't remember how I got free or how long it took. I had to rest often and was anxious to help Jim. I hurt my back several times trying to move when I couldn't. I remember my legs coming free, my feet still held tight and still thinking my crampons must be holding them, but knowing I wasn't wearing my crampons. My feet came free. I stood and realized I was down at the lower edge of the ice block. The edge that used to be in the middle half of the block was no longer there. I turned and ran up the slope to the top. I stood there looking at a strange new world. It was like walking on the roof of a building with no doors or windows. Avalanche ice was encrusted vertically against the ice block. There was nothing but a mass of rubble everywhere. I knew Jim was dead. I knew he died instantly. I knew it had taken me a long time to get out. I was overwhelmed with hopelessness. I tried to imagine where the tent was. I tried to imagine where Jim might be. I hit and kicked at the ice in the rubble. I tore the liner out of my helmet and tried to scrape the snow and ice. It was futile. I froze in fear when great gusts of wind roared down through the seracs above and the rocks on the canyon walls. It had changed. The morning had been calm. Now the wind was as loud as the thunder of avalanches. I went to the top of the ice block. There was a blue thing way out beyond in the rubble. I ran to it. It was a stuff sack with Jim's down gear. I found a ski, Jim's. With the ski I probed, but the chunks of ice made that useless. I kicked and scraped to dig. I cried. I prayed. I talked to Jim. I kept changing the place I dug. I couldn't figure out where anything had been. I probed. I looked around hoping to see something else. I kept digging, now in one place. I was getting nowhere. The wind was getting bad. I picked up the ski and stuff sack and walked away. After a while I stopped. I put the stuff sack where I could find it and went back. I probed and dug. I sat and cried. I said some things and left. I couldn't see very far, the wind was violent. I was walking in avalanche rubble for a long time. I would fall in gullies I couldn't see. I was confused. Down and out, I kept moving. I can't remember what I thought.

This was written by Douglas in his apartment after getting home. I arrived there the next afternoon, and he had already contacted the Army and the Alaska State Patrol. The latter agreed to fly three of us in to the lower part of the glacier. We left the following morning and flew in from Delta Junction. (See page 66)

(Left) The surface of the avalanche several days later. Douglas is visible, a vertical black mark standing in the top right corner of the photo near his tent site.
(Above) The ice block that Douglas got partly behind. He described it as big as a two-story house before the avalanche. It was buried this deep by the avalanche. The fellow in the photo was the third member of our team who flew with us in the State Patrol helicopter. I have not been able to find his name now, thirty-eight years later.

CHAPTER 1

THE BEGINNING

IT WAS A BRIGHT, sunny morning in September 1952 as the dozen or so members of the Washington Alpine Club (WAC) started the almost four-mile hike to Lundin Peak. For many of them, it would be the first real mountain climb after the climbing class. The trail up to Lundin started from the road just north of Snoqualmie Pass, went through heavy timber, around the south shoulder of Guye Peak, and then north into Commonwealth Basin. We climbed high on the side of Red Mountain and out of the timber that had hidden the view of Lundin from our sight.

Snoqualmie Pass summit area. The left peak is Snoqualmie Peak. Next, to the right, on the far skyline, is Lundin Peak. The rappel on Lundin was down the vertical face to the left of the highest point (photo on page 5). In the center foreground is the west face of Guye Peak. Commonwealth Basin is behind Guye Peak. Red Mountain is obvious to the right of Guye. Photo taken from a MAST helicopter returning from a mission 23 July 1977.

The usual route up Lundin Peak goes up to a pass on the ridge east of Lundin itself, then a scramble up the eight- to ten-foot-wide east ridge of Lundin. It was an easy scramble with a bit of walking up a slab, just enough exposure to height on each side of the ridge to give the beginners a feeling of real accomplishment when they reached the top. After a bit of lunch and a lot of picture taking on the summit, the party split, most of them returning the way they had ascended. A small group, five or six of us, took up an invitation by Bill Danilson, the leader, to go west a short distance from the summit and rappel to the bottom of the south face of Lundin. The rappel was about 110 feet to the bottom, using most of the length of the 120-foot manila climbing ropes of that era.

Bill set up a rappel anchor. The anchor consisted of several wraps of a piece of braided cotton rope around a large projecting rock. Each wrap went through a descending ring (a small iron ring) so that the multiple wraps provided support for the ring.

Left to right: Unknown lady, unknown male, Bill Danilson of WAC belaying someone on the rappel down the south face of Lundin Peak with Pete Steele feeding him the belay rope.

He then belayed each of us down the 110-foot rappel to the foot of the rock face. We had two climbing ropes, one to rappel on and one he used to give each of the party a belay as we descended.

When I got to the bottom (last of the group to rappel, except for Bill) and was off belay, Bill tied the two manila ropes together so he would have a double rope to rappel on, then leaned back to slide down the rope. In those days the dulfersitz rappel was the primary rappel method; there were no descenders or any other mechanical means used to control the speed of the descent. The friction of the rope around the body controlled the speed.

The usual descent was to push off with your legs and relax the tension on the rope that passed around your body so that you would have the freedom to drop ten to fifteen feet before increasing the tension on the rope and being pulled back to the cliff as you stopped. Then you would spring out again and drop a similar distance down the face, repeating this until you got to the bottom.

Lynn Buchanan rappelling. South face of Lundin Peak. 1952. Photo by Pete Steele.

In this case, Bill made the first drop and as he tightened his grip on the rope to swing back in, the anchor rope broke, dropping him in an increasing tangle of rope until he hit the rocks at the bottom of the cliff and bounced down thru the big boulders of the scree slope below. We rushed over to where he came to rest, many yards from the spot where he first hit. He was still alive but unresponsive when we got to him and there was not a lot that we could do. Several of us were ski patrollers and did what we could to keep him warm while we sent a couple of our party members to catch up with those on the regular descent route and send out a request for aid.

It was a long evening, sitting by Bill as he gradually went from unconsciousness to death on the warm summer evening. We could hear the cars going over Snoqualmie Pass and see the moon and stars shining brightly as we watched anxiously for the headlamps of the Mountain Rescue party. Many times we thought we saw them, but it was just the moon reflecting off the water of the mountain stream below. By the time the Mountain Rescue team arrived with a Bergtraga (an Austrian steel litter for carrying a patient, often referred to as the "Traga") Bill had died, so we helped with the evacuation through the night hours, arriving at Snoqualmie Pass at almost daylight.

The Bergtraga used in an MRC practice. (See also page 14)

I remained with Bill during the night and assisted in the carry-out. I went back the next weekend with Ome Daiber and several MRC members and assisted in the fact-finding climb to the scene of the accident followed by the rope evaluation. It was then that Ome talked me into joining Seattle Mountain Rescue Council (MRC). He suggested that I contact them during the week and get involved in the organization. I did, and the rest is history.

Lundin Peak. Aerial photo taken 20 October 2013.
The rappel was from the ridge just left of the summit.

There is an article about the accident in *Accidents in North American Mountaineering*, American Alpine Club (AAC), 1953.

My father, L. L. Buchanan, broke his spine late in the year 1951, and I had to drop out of my senior year at Washington State College (WSC) to work in the family business. I went to the Seattle terminal of Buchanan Auto Freight to manage the truck line. Working there, I joined the Washington Alpine Club

(WAC). WAC had a cabin on Snoqualmie Pass that was old at the time but is still there and has an active membership. They had a very active climbing and skiing program in addition to social events at the cabin. They taught a mountain climbing class each spring with lectures in Seattle, training sessions on Monitor Rock (a man-made climbing rock in a Seattle park) and various levels of training climbs, usually at Snoqualmie Pass. Monitor Rock was built of stone and concrete with many climbing routes built in and with belay rings imbedded in it during the construction.

Monitor Rock (now Schurman Rock), 1952.
Note the size of the trees.

Since the cabin at the pass was quite old and small, the members decided to enlarge it in the summer of 1952. One of my volunteer jobs for the construction was to rent an air compressor and jackhammer on several weekends, and then pull it to the Pass with my Jeep so we could break up the granite boulders around the cabin and put in the foundation for the new walls. The air compressor was as large and probably as heavy as the Jeep, an interesting sight going up Snoqualmie Pass.

Construction at the old cabin.

Construction at the old cabin.
The air compressor and the Jeep.

I joined MRC that summer and was qualified as a Rescue member shortly thereafter, based largely on the training I had received at WSC in Pullman from Bill Danilson. One of the requirements of membership in Mountain Rescue Teams was an Advanced First Aid card. I had taken that training at WSC in a Physical Education class; in fact, I had continued on and received training as a Red Cross First Aid Instructor. One of the students I had trained, and who was a Ski Patrolman at WSC, came to Seattle, joined MRC, and in a few years, became their First Aid Chairman. He created quite a fuss some years later when he made a motion at an MRC meeting to drop several members who had let their first aid training lapse. Since they had let that training lapse, the rules stated they should not be in MRC.

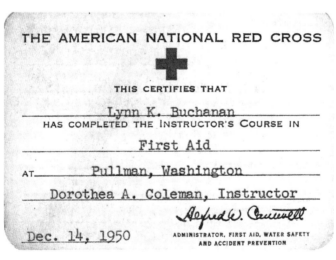

THE AMERICAN NATIONAL RED CROSS

THIS CERTIFIES THAT

Lynn K. Buchanan

HAS COMPLETED THE INSTRUCTOR'S COURSE IN

First Aid

AT_____Pullman, Washington

Dorothea A. Coleman, Instructor

Dec. 14, 1950   ADMINISTRATOR, FIRST AID, WATER SAFETY AND ACCIDENT PREVENTION

My original Instructor's First Aid card.

After the motion was seconded, someone asked who the culprits were. It turned out to be most of the very senior members—those who might show up at base camp or at the MRC meetings, but had not gone into the field for several years. In fact, it included most of the founding members of MRC! The motion was voted down and followed by another motion continuing those members in their rescue status, but without requiring them to keep their First Aid cards up to date.

I maintained an active membership in Seattle MRC for a year, then returned to WSC in January of 1953 to complete my last semester and graduate. After graduation, I was assigned to Ft. George Wright, an old US Army base west of Spokane, for my six weeks of Air Force ROTC summer camp. While there I got to fly both a C-47 and a C-45 for a half hour each as well as getting multiple rides in B-36 bombers (the Peacemaker). Following my graduation from summer camp and commissioning as a Second Lieutenant in the US Air Force, I returned to Yakima to work. In Yakima, Lex Maxwell, Bob McCall, Louie Newhall, and several others were organizing the first branch of MRC in the Eastern Washington area—the Central Washington unit of the Mountain Rescue Council. I eagerly participated in the organizing of the fledgling unit as it began its first year of operation.

In 1954, after several months of working with Buchanan Auto Freight in Yakima and participating with the Central Washington Mountain Rescue unit (CWMR in its later organization), I received my orders from the US Air Force to report for two years of active duty. While on active duty, I participated in several aircraft accident investigations in Okinawa and Taiwan.

When I returned to civilian life in Yakima in 1956, I resumed answering the callouts from CWMR. At one of CWMR's meetings, a representative of the Civil Air Patrol attended and told us of the advantages of merging with their group, formed during WW II. Since the CAP was mostly airplane oriented, the CWMR members were not too interested. Then he told us of the CAP dues structure. Since CWMR was primarily designed to help folks in trouble, they were not interested in joining another organization with an additional dues structure and more meetings. CWMR had our own goals to follow, so we bid the CAP representative farewell.

My nametag from the days CWMR was a unit of Seattle MRC.

After CWMR separated from MRC.

For many years, Seattle MRC was the only incorporated Mountain Rescue Team in the state. All the other teams participated as units of MRC and worked under their corporate heading for financial and operational expertise. Tacoma (TMRU) was the first to break away and incorporate as a separate unit, followed by all the others. CWMR remained part of MRC for many years, but it also eventually broke away and became the last to be incorporated separately.

Since I was working in the Seattle office of Buchanan Auto Freight fairly often, I maintained contact with MRC and was often called to participate with MRC as well as with CWMR on missions. Many Seattle missions required too much driving time to be useful, so after a few years, I dropped out of active participation in MRC. Since that time I trained as an EMT and as an IV Technician, as well as spending many weekends as a volunteer Avalanche Instructor with the White Pass Ski Patrol. Based on that, Seattle

MRC still called me for missions, usually high mountain missions, even when they were not calling other units.

Our name, Central Washington Mountain Rescue (CWMR), was adopted since we had members in Wenatchee, Ellensburg, and Yakima that worked together on missions, meetings, and training all up and down the east side of the Cascades. Mt. Stuart was a focal point for all three groups, since there were many accidents on that mountain over the years. Doctors Ralph Uber and George Roulston became members of the unit, participating in many missions with CWMR. Louie Ulrich, who moved to Yakima from Switzerland, and Marcel Schuster, who had been in the German Mountain Troops, were others who were on the perimeter of CWMR at that time.

As CWMR got more organized, Hal Foss, an insurance agent, joined, as did Dallas Hake, Jim Linse, John Thompson (a Deputy Sheriff at that time), and others. At one time, Hal was elected the president and I became the treasurer. When Hal went to Olympia to be the Director of Civil Defense (now the state's Emergency Services Department), I was elected president of the Central Washington Mountain Rescue Unit for a couple of terms.

The unit had many rescues in the years following that but except for Jim Linse's scrapbook, most of the records are missing for that period. A few of the more outstanding are detailed in the following chapters. I started keeping regular records after about sixteen years of activity.

In 1957, there was a rescue on the Mt. Adams Icefall that was written up in *The Iceworm*, a short-term newsletter telling some of the unit's activities (see the Addendum).

On 1 Sep 1957, Marvin Sundquist, Frank Slater, and I were on a late-season climb of Mt. Rainier when there was a crevasse accident above us on the Disappointment Cleaver route. The first we knew of it was when a Grumman Goose aircraft (SA-16) came growling low overhead looking for the accident site as we were climbing the Cleaver. We were dodging the rocks falling down the face of the Cleaver and saw the SA-16 drop a litter several hundred feet north of Disappointment onto the Emmons glacier. When we reached the top of Disappointment, we went out on the glacier to pick up the litter and bring it to the rock.

By the time we picked it up and carried it back for the park rangers and MRC folks who were climbing up to the rescue, it was too late to continue our climb, so we camped out at the top of the Cleaver. There was so much snow that year there was barely enough room for the three of us to sleep at the top of the Cleaver between the snow on one side and the cliff on the other, so we leveled a sleeping area—partly smooth sand and partly larger gravel. We had dinner, then spread our sleeping bags. Marvin had an air mattress, so he took the roughest part of the site and Frank and I had sand to sleep on. Shortly after we turned in under a nylon tarp for weather protection, we heard a *hissssss* coming from the air mattress. In a few minutes, Marvin was sleeping on rocks—the mattress had collapsed. While we were trying to sleep, more MRC folks and park rangers came by, picked up the traga, continued up to the accident site, and evacuated the body. The next day (after an almost sleepless night), the three of us cancelled our climb and returned to Yakima.

In his book, *The Challenge of Rainier*, Dee Molenaar devotes a chapter to the death of a climber named Haupert above Disappointment Cleaver on Labor Day weekend in 1957. In that chapter, Dee said his party of Mountain Rescuers met two of a party of four Austrians that had retrieved a stretcher dropped by a US Coast Guard plane. The paragraph above tells the story of the body recovery from the point of view of the three Yakima climbers (not Austrians). During my active duty time, I spent two months living across the street from the US Air Force Search and

Rescue (SAR) unit at Lowry Air Force Base, where the squadron of Grumman Goose (SA-16) aircraft warmed up both engines on every aircraft starting at 0500 each morning. Because of the experience, I was able to recognize the plane dropping the litter onto the glacier as it rumbled overhead, shaking lots of rocks loose above us on Disappointment Cleaver.

Mt. Rainier from above Sourdough Pass. Disappointment Cleaver is the rock ridge just right of the left skyline, between Little Tahoma and the summit. The angle of the sun shows the normal climbing route from Steamboat Prow as a darker gray line through the snow in the center of the photo where many climbers' footprints disturbed the surface.

CWMR ordered a Bergtraga ("traga") from Austria, the same as the one used by MRC. It was manufactured in two sections, had folding handles, and sported a wheel that fastened to the bottom for traveling over land with less energy needed from the carriers (see pages 4 & 14). There was skepticism expressed by several members about the wheel's usefulness on steep mountainsides, but after a body recovery (6 July 1961) in the Ellensburg Canyon, most of the skeptics were convinced.

The traga in use on a body recovery south of Dewey Lake. Judy Beehler (now Hanna) handling the traga. Jeans? It was late July, and this was the only snow encountered on the recovery. The wheel was attached after getting to the trail on bare ground.

That mission started as a search for an older man who had not returned home to Seattle the night before from a trip to the Ellensburg Canyon where he was searching for petrified wood. Several members of CWMR went to the location of his car, found in the canyon by a Yakima County Sheriff's Deputy. The car was parked on a turnout at the bottom of a shallow gully where a rudimentary trail led uphill. A hasty team of two members went up the trail to see if they could find any clues to his location. When they got up to some rock bands above the highway, they found his body where he had fallen from a ledge. The rest of the CWMR team took the traga and some ropes to the scene, secured the body into the traga, then started down the trail to the highway. The team members belayed the traga down the mountain, with only two members required to steady it on its wheel as they rolled it down to the vehicles. It was a lot better than carrying the fellow, and the team was convinced the traga was well worth what it cost.

John Thompson, who later became the Chief Deputy to Sheriff Bert Guns, was also a mountain climber. He joined CWMR in its early organization. That was the start of a long and profitable relationship for both Central Washington Mountain Rescue and the Sheriff's Office. CWMR maintained a room in the courthouse to keep our equipment and were called on to do all the rescues in Yakima County, as well as assisting other units in Eastern Washington on missions.

Since Central Washington Mountain Rescue was part of MRC for many years, CWMR was represented on the Seattle MRC Board first by Lex Maxwell, then after a few years, me. This involved a monthly trip to the board meetings, held in Seattle one evening a month. Since I was also on the White Pass Ski Patrol, I participated in the Pacific Northwest Regional Ski Patrol training sessions, which required another monthly trip over Snoqualmie Pass in the evening, returning after midnight, usually in the winter. The Ski Patrol lectures were at the University of Washington Medical School and were taught by Dr. Otto Trott, who taught both the MRC and the Ski Patrol much of their medical expertise.

After the national Mountain Rescue Association (MRA) was formed at Mt. Hood in 1959, membership in MRA was by units. MRA divided the units into regions and each region worked together. The Washington region included the units in the state and a couple of units from British Columbia (BC), Canada. The BC units almost never came down to a region meeting, so by the mid-1960s, talk started about making the units from Washington State into a separate region and not include the BC units. The BC units were advised but did not feel it was important enough to come down to meetings and join the units to their south. In response, the Washington units each picked a member to serve on an organizing committee.

Charlie Crenshaw of Seattle MRC was the chairman of the organizing committee. The committee held quite a few meetings planning, organizing, and writing the bylaws of the state organization, Washington Mountain Rescue Association (WMRA). I was the representative of the Central Washington units (Wenatchee, Ellensburg, and Yakima [CWMR]) on the committee. When the state association was finalized in 1970, Charlie was elected the first president of WMRA (1970 and 1971), and I was elected president two years later (1972 and 1973).

In 1966, Lisle Walker was hiking in one afternoon to climb the Mazama Glacier on the east side of Mt. Adams with the Portland Mazamas climbing club. He became ill as they camped for the night and got progressively worse. His party sent someone out to request aid, since they were unable to evacuate him. The Forest Service called the Yakima County Sheriff's Office (YSO), who then called Hal Foss and me. We went to my office and coordinated the operation from there. Since time was critical, we decided it would be faster if the Hood River Crag Rats (an Oregon Mountain Rescue [MORESCO] unit) did the evacuation. They were 100 miles closer to the accident scene. By the time the Crag Rats got to the scene on the glacier, Lisle had died, so they carried his body out to the road.

They later had a critique of the operation and invited CWMR to Hood River to attend it. They told CWMR that there was a problem brewing with their Sheriff about CWMR calling them out, rather than the Yakima Sheriff's Office making the call. We, CWMR and the Yakima Sheriff's Office, felt the operation went well, but the Hood River County Sheriff felt his office was not properly advised. John Thompson talked to Sheriff Bert Guns about the situation, then called Foss and me into his office, where we were sworn in as deputies. The Yakima County Sheriff's Office even had "Mountain Rescue" badges issued to Foss and me.

STATE OF WASHINGTON } ss.   **CERTIFICATE OF APPOINTMENT**
County of Yakima   I. _____ **BERT GUNS,**_____

Sheriff of Yakima County, State of Washington, reposing special confidence in
LYNN K. BUCHANAN

of ____ **Yakima** ____ in said County and State, do hereby deputize
and appoint him as SPECIAL DEPUTY SHERIFF OF YAKIMA COUNTY, in the State of Washington, to perform the particular acts only as Special Deputy as are hereinafter enumerated to be performed without pay, and revokable at my pleasure.

The particular acts to be performed by said Special Deputy Sheriff shall be as follows, to-wit: ____ **Unlimited** ____

Special Deputy for the above purpose AND NONE OTHER WHATSOEVER. It being distinctly understood that this appointment excludes said Special Deputy from exercising the power to levy any attachment or execution of any kind or character whatsoever, including the services of any Civil Process. 20

IN WITNESS WHEREOF, I have hereunto set my hand this _____ day of _____ **October** _____, 196 6 .

S-39   Sheriff of Yakima County, Washington

STATE OF WASHINGTON } ss.   **OATH OF OFFICE**
County of Yakima   I. **LYNN K. BUCHANAN,**

do solemnly swear that I am a citizen of the United States and of the State of Washington; that I will support the Constitution and Laws of the United States and the Constitution and Laws of the State of Washington, and will to the best of my judgment, skill and ability, truly, faithfully, diligently and impartially perform the duties of the office of Deputy Sheriff, in and for Yakima County, Washington, as such duties are prescribed by law, so help me God.

Subscribed and sworn to before me this ____ 20 ____ day of _____ **October** _____, 196 6 .

Notary Public

The original "Special Deputy (Unlimited)" ID card.

When CWMR went down to Hood River for the critique, everyone was cordial and chatted for a while to get acquainted. When the meeting got underway, the Hood River County Sheriff stood up and wanted to know why his office wasn't contacted by YSO. He felt that his constituents (the Crag Rats) were called out of *his county* to perform a rescue on Mt. Adams without the Yakima County Sheriff's Office doing the callout. That was not following what he thought was the proper protocol. After he got through, John Thompson got up and explained that he thought the Sheriff knew that it was two of the Yakima County Deputies that organized the mission. His office was totally involved by delegating the work to these two Deputies. The Hood River County Sheriff was very apologetic; he apologized for thinking that it was just two civilians, not Deputies from YSO, who had made the callout. He was sorry that he had even brought the subject up and thanked John for explaining how it did go through the proper channels.

That was the start of the Yakima County Sheriff swearing in at least one member of Central Washington Mountain Rescue as a deputy to be on scene as often as possible during rescues. This policy has been followed by every elected Sheriff, starting with Sheriff Bert Guns in 1966 and including Sheriff Ken Irwin to date (2010). When I completed the Yakima County Reserve Officers Academy in 1990 for a position in the Yakima Police Reserve, I was also issued a new County Sheriff's commission reflecting that.

For many years Central Washington Mountain Rescue (CWMR) was the only volunteer rescue group in Yakima County. We had a lot of interesting missions over many years. As the mission load picked up, someone in the Sheriff's Office decided to start an "Explorer Scout" chapter to handle searches, and even rescues, in the lowlands and when the weather was not too bad. CWMR provided much of the instruction for the young folks in the group but after a few missions, the Sheriff's Office was very specific that the Explorers could not participate in mountain work above the tree line nor where the terrain required mountain climbing skills and equipment. There were those in the Explorers that were not happy at being excluded on some missions, but a couple of accidents showed the reason. There was one young fellow who made a glissade down a snow slope on Mt. Adams, couldn't stop until he hit a rock, and was in the hospital for a while with a damaged kidney. Another was involved in a search on a steep, grassy mountainside near Fife's Peak when he slipped and didn't stop until he hit a tree, with resultant damage requiring hospitalization for a short while. In later years, Sheriff's Search and Rescue (SAR) has included many adults from many disciplines and has moved away from the Explorer Scout organization.

The officers of Central Washington Mountain Rescue organized the Yakima County SAR Advisory Council based on the King County organization (KSARA), and I was one of the first chairmen. The SAR Advisory Council included the Explorer Scouts, Sheriff's Posse, Ridge Runners (Jeeps), Ski Benders (snowmobilers), and others who had been needed on some missions, but attendance became sporadic at the meetings. After a few years, with less support from the Sheriff's Office, attendance fell off to a few diehards and the organization was disbanded. It didn't take long until the lack of an organization began to be noticed in both lack of unit cooperation on missions and in friction between units in the field, so the present SAR council was reformed by the Sheriff's Office on almost the same lines as the first one. It is still in operation, but with more emphasis from YSO.

Winter survival training near Ellensburg. Participants are building igloos and other snow shelters.

In the 1950s and '60s, there were annual Washington State Mountain Rescue conferences (training sessions) held, first at Snoqualmie Pass, but later in other locations, such as Blewett Pass on the east side of the Cascades and Mt. Erie, near Anacortes. They consisted of one or two days of seminar with an all-day Saturday outdoor training exercise. I was often a group leader or lecturer in these seminars, teaching subjects such as "Leadership," "Organizing the Search," "Avalanche Rescue," "Helicopter Safety," "Map & Compass," "Survival" and "First Aid." One of the highlights of this series was a winter training seminar where everyone camped out near Blewett Pass, building igloos and other snow shelters in which to spend the night.

Another exercise was on Snoqualmie Pass where Mountain Rescue had their first experience with a helicopter dropping supplies to a search team back in the rough terrain. It was a US Navy helicopter, and since they were not eager to land on snow to unload, they bundled the supplies in canvas, attached a ship's anchor to the bundle with a rope, and dropped it to the team. It hit, started to slide, then the flukes of the anchor dug into the snow and the bundle was retrieved by the team. The test was a success!

One of the first helicopters used in a practice on Snoqualmie Pass in the early 1950s. (Sikorsky SR-5).

In later practices and missions, where possible, the snow was foot-packed so the helicopter could land, as in the photo above. When the snow was loose and light, the helicopter hovered high enough to stay out of the billowing snow cloud.

Dallas Hake in front of the early CWMR truck on a winter mission.

In the summer and fall of 1958, Pete Steele and I, along with others from the Washington Alpine Club, climbed Lundin Peak several times to drill holes in the summit rock and place the above brass plaque on the summit. It was fastened to the rock with a new "glue" that someone obtained from Boeing called "epoxy."

In the summer of 2010, in e-mails with then president of the Washington Alpine Club, I was told that the plaque had been forcibly removed from the rock on the summit of Lundin Peak.

CHAPTER 2

MAST ADVENTURES

IN THE 1970s, the Military Assistance to Safety and Traffic (MAST) committee was formed in Washington State. This followed the original committee formed in Texas to facilitate the coordination of military assets, primarily the "Dust Off" helicopter units that began in the Korean War, with the civilian medical community. The many civilian vehicle accidents and other civilian injuries could be better cared for if there was more rapid transport from the scene of the accident to medical facilities. A state committee was formed with representation from the military and the medical community. It worked so well that other states followed suit, including Washington. Hal Foss, the state Director of Emergency Services (and a former Central Washington Mountain Rescue member), included a member of Mountain Rescue on the list as one of the required committee personnel. First a member of MRC, then myself as a member of CWMR, was selected to represent Mountain Rescue on the committee. It involved another monthly meeting, sometimes at Ft. Lewis, but often in Seattle. At the first meeting I attended, in Seattle, finding a parking space in the "U" district was a bit of a problem. I arrived at the meeting a bit late, just in time to hear Dr. J. Kranz, the president of the committee, announce that something had to be done about the "Yakima

Problem." I walked into the room just then and asked if they were talking about me? No, it was about all the letters the committee was receiving from Yakima residents wanting the services of the MAST helicopters. Both the committee and Senator Jackson were getting heavily lobbied. In the end, Senator Jackson solved the problem by telling the Army that they had to do something about it.

For the first few years after MAST was activated in Washington State, it operated out of Fort Lewis, the home of the 54th Medical Detachment (Helicopter). With first Hal Foss's and then my representation on the MAST committee and our encouraging the local people in Eastern Washington to write letters to Congress, particularly to Senator Jackson, the committee's "Yakima Problem" was settled by the Army with a MAST crew and helicopter located at the Yakima Firing Center through the summer season. As activity at the Yakima Firing Center (now Yakima Training Center) increased over the years, the MAST operation covered more and more of the year and eventually became a year-round function. This lasted until more medical helicopters were needed in Desert Storm, and the 54th Medical Detachment at Ft. Lewis was sent to the Middle East, to be replaced at the training center sporadically by other helicopter units. While the 54th Medical Detachment was providing the helicopters and crews at Yakima, CWMR members often went out to the Yakima Firing Center carrying desserts for evenings of conversation with the crews. On a couple of occasions, we were taken on helicopter missions down the valley, even given clandestine stick time in the Hueys.

Since Judy Beehler and I were fixed-wing pilots, the military pilots looked to us as ones who could be trained in more aspects of helicopter operation than folks with no flight experience. I have flown in several civilian helicopters starting back in the days of the Bell G-3. I have flown both UH-1 (Huey) and Kiowa (military Jet Ranger) helicopters, as well as riding as an observer/crewmember in them. I have also ridden as a crew-member in the Chinook (CH-47) and more recently in the UH-60. I was issued surplus crew equipment from army salvage to use on some missions. There was a large newspaper article and photo in the *Yakima Herald-Republic* when Judy Beehler was issued her very own helicopter helmet, (purchased from salvage by Seattle MRC) painted white and decorated with painted yellow daisies (painted by Jean, her sister) for use on Mountain Rescue missions.

Much of the year, I would fly my airplane to the meetings in Seattle or Ft. Lewis. To land at Ft Lewis, both for the meetings there and for the MAST standby weekends, I obtained permission to land at Gray Field on Ft. Lewis. Landing at an army airfield involved filling out several pages of military forms and buying extra insurance to cover the Army requirements. A side benefit of landing at Ft. Lewis was getting to practice ground-controlled approaches to landing, something most civilian instrument pilots never got to do unless they were prior service military pilots.

After serving on the MAST Committee for several years, I was elected in 1976 to the position of president of the committee for six years. During my participation on the MAST committee, I helped train many SAR units and Mountain Rescue personnel around the state to work around helicopters. I had been appointed to the committee just after the tragic death of an untrained nurse on a helicopter mission, so the committee became very active in publishing a training manual and conducting seminars for Mountain Rescue units and hospital personnel.

This involved many trips to those organizations, primarily on the west side of the state. I flew my Piper Cherokee on many of these trips, taking first Major Cloke, and later Major Wofford, (successive commanding officers of the 54th Medical Detachment) with me to some of the meetings.

*A MAST Huey hovering over the helicopter
pad at Harborview Hospital.*

Because of the many outdoor recreational opportunities in the Cascade Mountains of Washington State, the committee worked out an operational procedure whereby the Mountain Rescue teams maintained a two-person standby team at Ft. Lewis with the 54th Medical Detachment (Helicopter) (MAST) during the summer months. On weekends from May through September, Seattle MRC was the coordinating unit, ensuring that a trained Mountain Rescue team was at Ft. Lewis each weekend. CWMR did not want to participate as a unit, so Judy Beehler (now Hanna) and I spent three or four weekends each summer at Ft. Lewis as members of Seattle MRC.

The Mountain Rescue folks lived with the MAST crew for the weekend in three rooms on the second floor of a building just above the parking ramp for the Huey helicopters used by MAST. One room had three or four double bunks where the four crew-members and the two Mountain Rescue crewmembers slept. The rest of the time, we sat in the orderly room and read or watched TV until we were dispatched on a mission.

The training was invaluable to us, as were the number and type of missions we participated in. In July 1974 an accident near the summit of Mt. Stuart involved a Canadian climber with a broken pelvis. This was a ground mission for us, but our knowing the abilities and equipment of the MAST unit saved a lot of time and trouble for the injured folks on the mission. Seattle Mountain Rescue Council (MRC) and Central (CWMR) were the primary responders, but during the night approach, climbing the south side of Mt. Stuart in the dark, two CWMR members (Dave Rowland and Matt Kerns) were injured by rock fall just below the summit as they were waiting in the rain for daylight to arrive. Both CWMR and MRC personnel heard the rocks fall and one of our two teammates scream in pain. A large rock had hit him in the knee and dislocated his hip. He was not far from where several MRC members and I were sheltering under a large rock. At the first rumble of moving rocks, we leaped out from under our sheltering rock into the rain in case our rock moved. Paul Williams grabbed his radio and called base for more help, but unknown to him, the push-to-talk switch on the radio stuck. We left the radio while we dashed to the aid of the Yakima men.

Base heard no more information from those of us on the mountain except for the screams of the injured rescuer, so they started a massive callout of MRA teams. Not long after that, they had more than seventy Mountain Rescue people coming from all over the West Coast. As the sun came up, the cloud ceiling lifted a bit and two helicopters, one from the Yakima Firing Center and one from Fort Lewis, were able to reach the False Summit of Mt. Stuart to evacuate the injured Mountain Rescue folks from there. The landing zone was really tight, and one of the pilots was later heard wondering why he was hovering at 9,000 feet with one skid on the snow and the tips of his rotor blades only a couple of feet from a granite rock wall when he was just a few days away from his discharge from the Army.

Loading one patient into the helicopter on the False Summit of Mt. Stuart. The left skid of the UH-1 is hanging in the air, the right skid is partly on the snow ridge at 9,000 feet elevation.

After the injured Mountain Rescue folks were safely evacuated from the False Summit of Mt. Stuart, the rest of us climbed up to the injured climber from British Columbia, who was originally the reason we had been called. After the patient was removed from his tent and it was safely stowed, a helicopter returned and hovered over the patient while the crew lowered a Stokes litter from the helicopter on climbing ropes. The patient was placed in the litter and carefully lashed in by the Mountain Rescue Team. He was then airlifted from the shelf carved from the snow just below the summit where he had spent the night.

Someone took a photo of the helicopter leaving Mt. Stuart from just below the summit (at 9,100 feet) with the climber in the litter hanging beneath the helicopter as it descended to the pass on the other side of the valley. That picture was on the front page of the *Seattle PI* newspaper the next morning and ended up on the desk of the Commanding General of Ft. Lewis.

The troops at the MAST detachment had been instructed not to transport persons outside the helicopter, nor were they to use the winch on the helicopter unless it was a life or death situation. The crewmembers of that helicopter were summoned to the Commanding General's office the next morning to explain the photo on the front page of the newspaper. They told the general that it was a life or death situation and he could call me in Yakima for verification. The general picked up the telephone and called right then. I, in my office in Yakima, explained to the general how a ground evacuation off that extremely steep snow slope would have been very risky and could have caused multiple injuries or death if anything went wrong. Due to the steepness of the slope, there was no way to put the injured climber inside the helicopter until the crew got him to a lower elevation where they could land. It was a good conversation about the pros and cons of helicopter evacuation. The general thanked me for the discussion.

A few hours later, I got a call from the pilot thanking me for my conversation with the general. The flight crew had been looking at being suspended from flight status by the general until he had the discussion with me and was satisfied that the crew had acted properly.

The story of that rescue was written up and published in *SAR Magazine* by Paul Williams of Seattle MRC. There were several photographs by me and about a five-page story describing what Paul characterized as the most strenuous mission in his twenty-five years of MRC history to that date.

❖ ❖ ❖

On 18 July 1976, Judy Beehler and I were on standby in the MAST "hootch" at Gray Field, Ft Lewis, when we were dispatched to a climbing accident at Lena Lake on the Olympic Peninsula. The location was well known to the pilots of the MAST helicopters because it was close to a trail that led to The Brothers, a popular mountain climb in the Olympics. Beehler and I had been on a mission to that lake on 13 July 1975, just five days more than a year prior. That had been a similar accident.

In this case a young man had fallen while climbing and sustained a severe gash to his leg. His climbing companions were assisting him down to the lake after someone had run out to civilization and phoned the Sheriff, who then requested a MAST pickup.

The lake had steep banks and tall trees on all sides except for where the supply stream came down the mountain and flowed into the lake. The stream had, over many years, carried sand and gravel into the lake and made a very small peninsula that extended into the lake. The grass and small brush on the peninsula allowed the Huey to land on that patch of gravel and under the branches of the nearest tree. The pilot hovered down over the surface of the lake, then slowly hovered to the shore where he could put his skids on the gravel while the tail rotor extended over the water. An interesting pickup! When the injured climber was on board with the crew, the pilot started the rotor and when all was ready to fly, he lifted off, backed over the lake surface, climbed over the surrounding trees, and departed for the hospital with the patient.

❖ ❖ ❖

In October of 1976, the National MAST Conference was held in Seattle. As chairman of the Washington State MAST committee, I was in charge of preparing for the conference, but since it conflicted with a national MRA meeting, I had to leave Seattle the morning the MAST conference started. I did get to meet guest speaker William Christopher (Father Mulcahy of TV's *MASH*). I welcomed him to Seattle and had coffee with him the evening he arrived. The meeting preparations were good and the conference was a success.

The standby weekend of 23 July 1977 was launched with a mission where Beehler and I accompanied the MAST crew from Ft. Lewis to pick up a Boy Scout with a broken ankle. He was hiking with his troop along a ridge northwest of Snoqualmie Pass, many miles from the road, when a large rock slid onto his foot and ankle, breaking the fibula. His buddies got the rock off his foot and one of them was able to radio for help. The mission was pretty straightforward; the Scouts were high enough on the ridge to provide a great landing zone (LZ) for the helicopter. As the Huey was lifting off from the LZ, the pilot got a radio call for another mission involving an elderly man with a heart attack at Spectacle Lake, northeast of Snoqualmie Pass. Because of the critical nature of the problem, the helicopter was diverted directly to the lake with the one patient already on board. This was before the days of GPS, so it was particularly helpful to the pilot to have mountain climbers on board who knew the locations of the peaks, trails, and lakes.

Unfortunately, the fisherman had expired before the helicopter arrived. MAST had a rule that they were not to pick up bodies, but after looking at the trail out of Spectacle Lake, the pilot decided that an exception should be made. The Huey was there and a carryout on foot would be both hazardous and take a lot of time getting down that steep trail beside the waterfall and travelling many miles to the nearest road.

Part of Spectacle Lake from about 500 feet above it. The trail to the lake comes in along the waterfall outlet from the lake at the center of the right side of the picture. The MAST Huey landed on one of the granite outcrops just left of the outlet of the lake.

The body was loaded on board and the pilot started the climb out of the tight valley that surrounded Spectacle Lake. When the helicopter was high enough to clear the surrounding ridges and leveled out to fly toward Snoqualmie Pass, a loud banging started on the starboard outside of the Huey. The previous photo shows how few places there were to park a helicopter in that area. The pilot pulled the nose of the Huey up to slow the forward speed as he looked for a place to land. The banging stopped. Then someone noticed that the buckle and part of the waistband of a pack was hanging outside of the closed door of the helicopter. Open door! Pull belt inside! Close door! Resume forward speed to Snoqualmie Pass. The body was left with the civilian authorities there, and the MAST bird proceeded on to

Harborview Hospital to leave the injured Boy Scout before returning to Ft. Lewis.

View to the west (Mt. Thompson) while the helicopter was climbing out of Spectacle Lake. The Pacific Crest Trail is visible along this side of the ridge from high on the slope to the right to the pass on the left side of the picture. Snoqualmie Pass is over the ridge and down to the left.

On 12 August 1979, after one of the more interesting missions Mountain Rescue participated in, Judy Beehler and I were awarded citations from the Army through the 54th Medical Detachment. On that mission, launched from Fort Lewis, a very ill patient in the hospital in Port Townsend needed transport by a MAST helicopter to Harborview Hospital in Seattle. The helicopter was restricted to fly between the hospitals at almost sea level altitude. The helicopter flew so low over Puget Sound that, when they found a barge in their way they had to climb to get over it, then went back down to their sea skimming altitude. While en route, the patient's heart stopped.

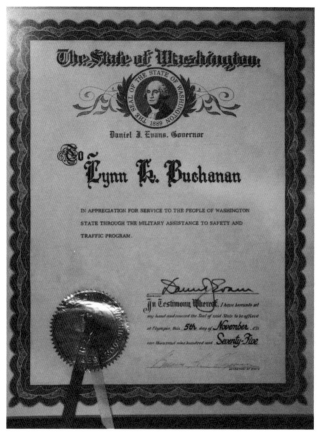

On 5 November 1975, while president of the MAST committee, I was invited to Olympia to receive, in a public ceremony in the rotunda of the Washington State Capitol building, a personal commendation from Governor Dan Evans for my efforts in the coordination of civilian and military personnel in saving lives in the State of Washington.

The crew, including the two of us, had to work rapidly to get CPR started and continued in order to keep the patient alive until we arrived at the Harborview helipad. The landing at the helipad was the highest altitude the helicopter achieved on the entire flight after picking up the patient. The Harborview ambulance crew continued the CPR that we had started until the patient arrived in the emergency room.

DEPARTMENT OF THE ARMY

CERTIFICATE OF ACHIEVEMENT

AWARDED TO

LYNN K. BUCHANAN
Seattle Mountain Rescue

On August 12, 1979, while serving as a crewmember with the 54th Medical Detachment M.A.S.T. on an Aeromedical Evacuation mission; Mr. Buchanan exemplefied himself as an outstanding member of Seattle Mountain Rescue. While enroute from Port Townsend to Seattle, Washington, an extremely critical patient on board suffered a complete Cardio-Respiratory failure. With immediate response Mr. Buchanan came to the aid of the flight medic to assist with CPR on the patient. Once the patient was stabilized, Mr. Buchanan helped to assure the safety of the aircraft as it landed at Harborview Medical Center in Seattle as an awaiting ambulance crew stood by for the patient transfer. Mr. Buchanan's ability to act immediately and to integrate with the crew in order to save the patient, makes him a credit to the 54th Medical Detachment, Seattle Mountain Rescue, and the United States Army. Your services are greatly appreciated.

August 21, 1979
DATE

COMMANDING

My certificate from the US Army after the mission described above. Judy Beehler received a similar certificate.

Another time when Beehler and I were sitting in the "hootch" at Gray Field on a Saturday afternoon, the word came in for a mission in the South Olympic Mountains. A climber had fallen on a peak called Shark's Fin. The ridge was very steep-sided and narrow on top with no place for landing a helicopter (no LZ). The other climbers had gotten the injured fellow off the "Fin" but didn't have the equipment to transport him to an LZ. It was decided that the crew would have to locate a good LZ and use the military Stokes litter to transport the injured fellow.

The crew launched, flew to the Fin, and looked for a spot to land. The ridge itself was a real knife-edge. The Fin was just a higher spot on the ridge. There was a flat spot with a clearing in the trees on the west side about 1,000 feet below the top of the ridge, so the pilot put the Huey down there and the two Mountain Rescue folks with the medic and crew chief began the climb to the ridge top. The gulley they were ascending was full of snow, so the two climbers carried the litter and some blankets while kicking steps so the other two could follow behind with reasonable safety.

When we got to the top of the ridge, we discovered that the trail to the area was just a few feet below the top of the ridge on the other side, running parallel to the ridge top. The trail was the only flat spot anywhere near. There the medic checked the patient, who had a rather serious leg fracture, then we splinted his leg and placed him in the litter. We placed plastic in the bottom of the litter to keep the patient dry, then wrapped him in the blankets to try to keep him warm. Sliding him down to the Huey in the litter was a long, difficult job. The snow helped, but the slope was steep enough that the litter had to be belayed by one of the climbers while the other three members of the team pulled it downhill or carried it around stumps and large rocks sticking up through the snow.

The afternoon was long and was getting close to dark before the patient was loaded into the Huey. When we reached the helicopter, the pilot told us that the valley was so narrow and steep-sided that he had been out of radio contact with Ft. Lewis ever since calling them to report that we had an LZ and were descending into it.

As soon as the patient was secured in the Huey, the pilot lifted off. When he was high enough to have radio contact, he reported that they were inbound with the patient. The MAST base at Ft. Lewis told him that the helicopter had been out of contact for so long that they had already sent a second crew to the scene in search of us. The second crew turned around, and we flew to a Tacoma hospital with the injured man before returning to Ft. Lewis and a long delayed dinner.

On another MAST mission out of Ft. Lewis, a horseman was injured in Olympic National Park. One of his companions had ridden out and reported that he was at one of the old park shelters on a main trail so he would be easy to spot with enough room near the shelter for a good LZ. The Park Service had called this mission in and said they had a park ranger standing by near a south entrance to the park to guide the pilot to the shelter.

We landed at the designated road end to pick up the ranger. The ranger had a map of the park, but admitted he had never flown over the park before. The pilot just had to fly up "that" trail, which started over in "that" corner of the parking lot, and it would lead us right to the shelter. The pilot made his takeoff then asked the ranger to show him where the trail went from that point. The ranger was unable to see the trail under the dense forest of Olympic Park. He told the pilot that the shelter had to be on the other side of "that" peak, pointing to one of the many peaks in the Olympic Mountains. The pilot flew there and around it, but there was no clearing below. The ranger said, "Maybe it is that one," pointing at another peak. No clearing or shelter was on that peak either. He allowed that the country sure looked a lot different from up there; he was used to seeing it from the ground.

About that time, the pilot (rather impatiently) told the ranger to give his helmet to me and when I was on the intercom, he asked if I had any idea where the shelter was or were they going to have to go back for fuel. My USGS map showed the trail crossing a low pass near the first peak, so I directed the pilot to it. The pass was high enough that there were no trees on it and the trail was visible. With that and the elevations visible on the

USGS map, it was an easy matter to direct the pilot in the direction the map indicated. By comparing the peaks in the vicinity with the USGS map, we flew to the shelter. At the shelter the patient was given medical care by the medic, loaded on board, then flown to Harborview after dropping the ranger at the park entrance. We then flew back to Ft. Lewis with another mission accomplished.

On another occasion I was flying the commanding officer of the detachment, Major Cloke, to a meeting with some hospital folks over on the coast in my Piper Cherokee. I was shuffling charts and other papers as I was flying, keeping track of my route across the southern part of the Olympic Peninsula. Major Cloke commented that I really needed a kneeboard to keep my paperwork organized while flying. When we were back at Ft. Lewis after the trip, he called me and several of the crewmembers into the dispatch room and entertained them all with an elaborate speech about how a civilian pilot shuffles paperwork while flying. Then he produced an Army kneeboard, which he said was from salvage, and presented it to me to use while on the committee and flying MAST personnel in my civilian aircraft. When he wanted it back, he would ask for it. He was making the public presentation so everyone would know where it came from and when I was to return it.

The Mountain Rescue standbys started in the days of all male pilots and continued into the days of female flight crewmembers. One day the Mountain Rescue team arrived at the MAST "hootch" and we were introduced to a new co-pilot, a female. Army policy had changed.

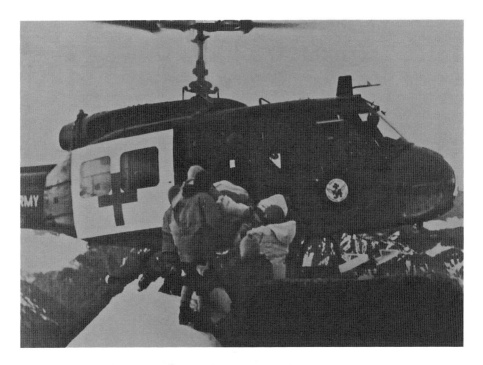

Lynn Buchanan, Mountaineer
In service to the sick and injured
In the chair and in the field
Chairman, Washington M.A.S.T. Committee
1976~1982

Photo with the inscription presented to me upon my retirement from the MAST committee in 1982. This is the photo I took with Dallas Hakes's camera in 1974 on the Mt. Stuart rescue detailed on page 27.

One of the crewmembers told us that shortly after her arrival a senior officer walked into the "hootch" on a surprise inspection. He found the crew sitting in the easy chairs watching the TV in the corner with their backs to the door. All were sitting comfortably with their heads leaning back on the top of the chairs while they waited for another rescue call.

The officer walked up to them and demanded to know why "this soldier" had not gotten a haircut recently! Someone looked around, saw the rank of the officer, and called, "Ten-hut!" Everyone leaped to their feet and faced the officer. When the female pilot, who stood more than six feet tall and with longer hair than the males, turned around, the officer realized her hair was regulation length for a female. He had not expected to see a female pilot.

He continued his inspection and looked in to the sleeping room—four double bunks. He asked the crew chief, who was just barely minimum height for the army, "Where does the female sleep?" His response was, "Wherever she wants to, SIR!" Each crewmember pulled a twenty-four-hour duty day, sleeping when they had time, and then went home for a couple of days off before returning to regular duty. The MAST crews had very few nights of uninterrupted sleep.

❖ ❖ ❖

Ft. Lewis in June 1979. Almost a hundred helicopters appeared to be on the field in those days.

❖ ❖ ❖

Those of us in CWMR often went out to the MAST building at the Yakima Firing Center in the evening to sit around and shoot the breeze with the MAST crew. We would usually take some cake and ice cream and spend an entertaining evening with them. There was one summer evening that we were out there until almost dark chatting with the crew when one of them reminded the pilot that he had to go to Walla Walla and pick up their credit card. They had left it when they fueled there earlier in the day. The pilot asked if we wanted to go along. Of course we did.

As the crew was doing the preflight on the Huey, the pilot asked if I would like to fly the bird down to Walla Walla. He knew that we were both pilots and each had a bit of stick time in Hueys. He was rated as an instructor pilot and said he would see how I did. I was really happy to get some more time at the controls. He had me get in the right seat, the Pilot in Command (PIC) seat in a Huey. After he started it, I lifted off to a hover, following his instructions. The Huey was a bit squirrelly in the hover. I asked if he was going to turn on the switch that dampened the controls, taking out some of the squirrelly feeling. He laughed, commented on my knowing about that switch, and turned it on. As things calmed down, he had me start climbing out of the airport area and we were off to Walla Walla. After a little over an hour of flying time, we arrived at the airport there where he requested a landing in the middle of the airport. He had called the fueling office and told them about needing to pick up the credit card so they were ready to meet him (he gave them some excuse why they had to drive out where there were no lights; they bought it). After we landed, I quickly changed seats with the crew co-pilot and the fuel truck came out to refuel us. After we refueled, Judy was asked to fly us back to Yakima. It was a very interesting evening spent at the Firing Center.

Here are the hangars at Ft. Lewis several years later with two Hueys to the left of the farthest hangar, just this side of the tower. There is a Blackhawk, two Chinooks, and another Blackhawk visible on this side of the Hueys.

54th Med. Huey with the crew holding the doors open for the pilot and co-pilot. 1979.

All good things must come to an end. In 1982 the Commanding General of Ft. Lewis decided the MAST committee was not necessary in its current form, so it was cut down in size and composed of just a few folks meeting sporadically at Ft. Lewis. As the colonel stated, "The political scene has changed, and we don't need you civilian volunteers anymore." I retired from the committee and was given a framed photo and the commendation that accompanied it shown on page 39. The back of the photo has the signatures of all of the committee members.

CHAPTER 3

TRAINING AND MISSIONS

IN ORDER TO BE a member of a Mountain Rescue team, one must first be a mountain climber. The ability to get into severe terrain and back out again safely is something one has to learn for themselves first, before volunteering to help others. It may look easy on most rescues, but without the basics of safe mountain climbing skills, there are going to be those rescues that challenge even the most experienced climbers. All mountain climbs are training for the ability to get into severe terrain and return with an injured person without causing more damage to the patient or any damage to the rescuer.

All Mountain Rescue Teams, including CWMR and Seattle Mountain Rescue (SMR, formerly MRC), routinely practice what they will work with in the field. The majority of practice sessions are done locally, because that is where most of our missions really happen; however, there are occasions when we are called to work in unfamiliar areas. The Mountain Rescue Association (MRA) spring national conferences are held in different parts of the United States with different terrain features each year, which also broadens our experience. In addition, the states of Washington and Oregon each have several volcanoes that have many glaciers on them, so on occasion the local teams make a practice trip to

Mt. Rainier or Mt. Adams to practice on glaciers and at higher altitudes for the missions that require familiarity with that terrain.

There was a time that a call was made for team members with high altitude training who were needed for a rescue on Mt. McKinley and another time when the US Air Force needed ground search teams in really wet, cold, snowy weather next to the Canadian border in Washington. It is for times like this that we practice with other teams in terrain that may be common for them, but not so common for us.

Both CWMR and SMR teams have practiced in joint training sessions in Mexico that had two goals: getting team members used to working at higher altitudes than we have here in Washington, and working with members of Socorro Alpino, the Mexican Mountain Rescue Team, to make joint operations work more smoothly.

High on Popocatepetl, left to right, back row: Lynn Buchanan, Lee Henkle, Ome Daiber, Dave Rowland, and Jim Martin. Left to right, front row: Judy Beehler, Matie Daiber, Sherry Rowland. 1974.

In addition, we have had a few opportunities for team members to go to other countries for experience working in other types of terrain, high altitude peaks, or deep winter, arctic conditions. Winter conditions on Mt. Rainier, even some summer conditions in Alaska, for example, are very similar to conditions in the Arctic, thus the Arctic expedition to Baffin Island.

The first mission to Mexico, organized by Seattle MRC and sponsored by Eddie Bauer and a few other manufacturers, was in 1974, where several members climbed one or more of the following peaks: Popocatepetl (17,855'), Iztaccihuatl (17,312'), and Pico de Orizaba, the highest peak in Mexico at 18,701 feet. I was on a team that reached the summit of Popocatepetl on that trip. While there, the Mountain Rescue folks worked out of the lodge at Paso de Cortez with the Socorro Alpino team on rope work, handling litters, and first aid.

Judy Beehler, Lynn Buchanan and two members of the Brigada de Rescate/Socorro Alpino, the Mountain Rescue group of Mexico City. They are at the summit (but out of the wind) on Popocatepetl (17,888 feet). Behind Judy, the crater wall dropped vertically almost 1,000 feet to the bottom of the crater. 1974.

❖ ❖ ❖

In early 1978, Steve Trafton of Seattle MRC invited me to participate in a winter climb north of the Arctic Circle on Baffin Island in northeastern Canada with him and three other members of MRC: Al Errington, Jim Shed, and Martin Waller, plus one member from Olympic Mountain Rescue, Brad Albro. This would give us the experience of living outdoors in really severe cold weather and being able to travel and climb mountains without the ability to retreat to the comfort of civilization when things got tough. In the first few days after arriving at Clyde River on Baffin Island, we made a few purchases from the Hudson Bay store, met with the local Inuit town council, then arranged for a nearly seventy-mile snowmobile transport to where we planned to live and climb. We spent seventeen days living on the ice and made the first ascent (first time it was climbed) of Broad Peak, a spectacular 6,150-foot rock tower on the edge of a frozen fjord.

Broad Peak (center) on Baffin Island. Our route in was up the lateral moraine on the left side of the glacier after we got off the frozen fjord in the foreground.

After climbing Broad Peak, we had to endure a three-day storm, eating and sleeping in our tents. Occasionally we would have to go outside to dig the snow away from the lee side of the tent where it was piling up and pushing the side of the tent in. When the storm stopped, five of us went out to try to climb a second, smaller, peak in an afternoon. The climb ended with all five of us being carried off the peak in a massive avalanche that deposited us on the glacier in the valley below. That gave us a bit more understanding of avalanches, a hazard of winter travel, than we really wanted to experience!

My memories of the trip down in the avalanche are rather vivid—as one who had a lot of training and had read a lot of first-person stories of rescues and body recoveries—I was wondering how anyone could even think of swimming while rolling end over end down the mountain. The soft slab blocks were pummeling me but with all the other sensations going on, I don't remember them being painful. They just kept me from doing anything really constructive with my arms or legs. I was thinking about getting myself to the top of the mass, but it was truly difficult to know where I was in relation to up and down as I tumbled inside the snow mass. I could remember pictures of bodies dug out and wanted to avoid that, but there was really little that I could do, constructive or otherwise.

Everyone survived the avalanche, but some of our climbing equipment was lost, so we spent the next week or so exploring and hiking into the high valleys of the Arctic coast. When the Inuit picked us up at the end of our time on the ice, we traveled by snowmobile and sled back to Clyde River to await our flight back to civilization. The highest temperature recorded on the trip was ten degrees above zero (F) just one day before we started back to the United States. (I printed the story on my computer in 2009 for a few of us. Steve Trafton privately printed a large, hardcover book about the trip also.)

Digging out of the avalanche. When the avalanche stopped, everyone was partly exposed. Those who could, helped the others get free of the snow. Steve Trafton on the left, wearing one of the parkas designed for the expedition by Eddie Bauer Company; next, Al Errington, then Brad Albro in the red shirt. Behind Albro is Martin Waller.

In 1995, seven of the CWMR members repeated the trip to Mexico, first climbing Nevada de Toluca (15,433 feet) with Rubin Garcia, one of the members of Socorro Alpino, travelling from a hotel in Mexico City. He went with the CWMR folks to what he called the summit, a hundred feet below the real summit, claiming the last few feet were rather dangerous. I had climbed Toluca with Consuelo Herrara on a business trip to Mexico City a year or two prior to this trip. She and I had climbed the outside of the crater rim to the summit, a much more interesting route. On the 1995 trip, I insisted on going to the real summit again and told Rubin that I had climbed there with Consuelo (female and close to seventy years old). Betty Martinsen insisted that if I could go, she was going also. We then finished the climb to the top. It was really not difficult.

Lynn and Betty on the summit of Toluca.
Photo: Ruben Garcia

We got permission to go to Paso de Cortez between Popocatepetl and Iztaccihuatl for acclimatization to altitude and to stay in the Socorro Alpino room in the ITT building there. Popocatepetl was off limits due to the active eruption it was undergoing at that time.

Iztaccihuatl (17,312 feet) from the ITT building.

Popocatepetl (Popo) from the approach to Iztaccihuatl.

Four of the team: Betty, Joe Roemer, Jeff Main, and Mike Chadwick climbed to the summit of Iztaccihuatl from there. Then, after a brief return to Mexico City, we all went to Pico de Orizaba, which was climbed by Betty, Terry Sinclair, Jeff, Rubin, Jorge, Connie, and me.

Jeff Main, Ruben (Socorro Alpino), Lynn Buchanan, Mike Chadwick, Betty Martinsen, Joe Roemer, and Terry Sinclair. Socorro Alpino headquarters room at the ITT (International Telephone and Telegraph) station near Paso de Cortez. Photo by Connie Smithhisler (now Buchanan).

The climb of Orizaba was accomplished in spectacularly clear weather. Two members of Socorro Alpino (Ruben and Jorge) accompanied all of us CWMR members on the climb after providing the transportation from Mexico City. They told us of a German climbing team that had fallen over a thousand feet down the hard ice from the summit, killing one and seriously injuring the rest just a couple of weeks before.

Jorge drove his father's Chevrolet van with everyone aboard (plus all the climbing equipment on the roof) to Orizaba from

Mexico City. A stop for dinner was made at the Casa Blanca restaurant in Tlachichuca. From there, Jorge followed often very faint roads to within one to one and a half kilometers of the climbing hut at 14,000 feet elevation. He was well above timberline before he encountered some deep sand and decided the team could carry their packs the rest of the way to the hut.

El Pico de Orizaba (center), from a yard in Tlachichuca.

The hut had a table for cooking inside to the left as one goes in the door (page 56), and three layers of wooden shelves were to the right. These shelves served as places to sleep with everyone lying side by side and with their heads or feet against the right wall. It was dark (2230) when the team arrived, but there was room for everyone on the sleeping shelves. After a few bites of food, everyone climbed into their sleeping bags for a good night's rest.

We all spent the next day hiking in the vicinity of the hut to get better acclimatized to the altitude. The following day Joe did not feel like climbing, but the rest of the team were up before daylight and started up the mountain. A thousand feet or so above the hut, just below the bottom of the snowfield, Mike was not feeling too energetic, so he returned to the hut. At the snowfield, which continued to the summit, everyone roped up, put on our crampons and climbed up the hard frozen snow and ice. Jeff and Ruben were on one rope, Betty and Terry on another.

Loading the van in Mexico City. L to R: Joe Roemer, Ruben (on top), Jeff Main, Mike Chadwick (on the bumper), Betty Martinsen, and Terry Sinclair.

They were the fast teams, a bit faster than Connie, Jorge, and me on the other rope. Jorge said he would be old someday also, "So let's go slower".

The crater of Orizaba was similar to the one on Popocateptl with vertical walls to the bottom of the crater. There was a sandy patch of ground extending fifteen to twenty feet from the edge of the crater back to the two to four foot vertical wall of snow. When Connie and I reached that spot, the rest of the team were resting on the "beach." They had been to the summit and back, so both of the young Mexican climbers were encouraging us to continue on to the summit, only a few hundred feet away around the rim. From that distance, who would not complete the climb?!

Of course! It was a stroll on the snow with a few sandy patches along the rim of the crater (at 18,701 feet) with Ruben going along to take a few pictures. The highest summit for either one of us had been accomplished!

The climbers' hut (Octavio Alvarez) at Piedra Grande (14,000 feet) on Orizaba.

Then it was time to return. The glacier ice and the snow covering it was hard and solid but rough on the surface, so it required careful walking with our crampons on the way down. It was, however, much easier than the climb up. With the rough surface, it was easy to see how the German team had gotten into trouble a couple of weeks before, perhaps just a little stumble, a fall, then a long tumble down the steep rough ice.

The route to the summit. There is an old abandoned irrigation canal below the cliff on the right, and in the center of the photo is another hut (Augusto Pellet) on the route.

The summit from the lower part of the snowfield. The first two rope teams of two each are in the distance, looking like only three climbers. From back to front on our rope are Lynn, Connie, and Jorge. Photo by Mike Chadwick.

The crater of Orizaba (from "the beach" on the left).

On the team's return from the summit of Orizaba, a TV crew was interviewing a famous Mexican climber, Ricardo Torres, at the lodge (14,000 feet). They were asking him about his climb of Everest some time previously. When Ricardo saw the CWMR team returning, he referred the TV crew to us to give our story of the climb to the summit of Orizaba that very day. The total time for our climb was thirteen hours from the hut to the top and back.

It was still daylight when everyone returned to the hut, so we gathered our gear and hiked down to the van. We then drove down to Puebla so everyone could spend the night in a hotel bed. En route, we stopped in Tlachichuca to see if we could get some food in the restaurant where we had eaten on the way to the mountain. The town (and the restaurant) was pretty well closed up, but there was a fellow with a taco stand on the street that was selling small, six-inch tacos and tortillas with meat, cilantro, and salsa. He had slices of cooked meat stacked on a vertical spit that was heated by a gas flame playing on the meat. As the proprietor got an order, he sliced some meat off the edges of the stack into his hand and put it on a tortilla. The two Mexican fellows decided that was good enough for them, so they stopped to eat. I decided that if I got sick, I would be in the United States in a day or so, so I tried a couple of the tacos, but with just the meat and the salsa. They cost a peso each. They were good!

Connie and Lynn Buchanan on the summit of Orizaba (18,701 feet). Photo by Ruben Garcia. (Note the whiteness in the photos above the crater. That was not visible to the eye when we were there. See also the photos on pages 47 and 58.)

The next day, Mike and the two Mexican fellows went back to Mexico City in the van while the rest of us rode a new Mercedes Benz bus to Vera Cruz for a day or two in the tropical sun, sightseeing and enjoying some good eating. After arranging for hotel rooms for that night, we all went down to the beach to wade in the warm salt water with our boots, strings tied together, hanging over our shoulders. We went from 18,701 feet to sea level in twenty-four hours!

After cleaning up from the climb, and wading in the ocean, we all went to a restaurant on the beach for a seafood dinner—mostly orders of large shrimp—then we went back to the hotel for the night. In the morning, the ladies went downtown to do some shopping, and I went to the beach to watch some surf fishing. A boat took a net out into the surf, dropped it into the water, and then the folks on shore pulled the net in. Quite a crew was pulling the net in and collecting the fish. They tossed the bigger fish into the buckets and the small ones out onto the sand for the seagulls to eat.

Fishing in the surf.

When the team was all back together, we had breakfast, then walked through the city, sightseeing. This was where the United States Marines had invaded Mexico, many years ago, then marched to Mexico City and conquered it. (Thus, the phrase in the US Marine hymn, "From the Halls of Montezuma.") It was a big city then, much bigger now. There is a fort in the harbor that they had to conquer before landing in the city. We came down a highway from Mexico City, but it must have been a long march from Vera Cruz for the marines. In addition to the distance, they had to climb from sea level to 7,000 feet, the elevation of Mexico City.

After more sightseeing and another night in the hotel, we returned to Mexico City. From there we flew to Denver, where we went through customs, followed by another long flight home and back to work for everyone.

On that trip to Mexico, each member of the party succeeded in climbing two of the high peaks. For me that was Nevada de Toluca for the second time (the first for Connie). Then Connie and I each made our first climb of Pico de Orizaba (18,701 feet).

I have participated in more than 300 missions with the various Mountain Rescue units, as well as a few missions that occurred while on a climbing trip or resulted from a phone call requesting help in other places. Some of them are included on the following pages.

On 18 November 1963, a search started for two crewmen who had to eject from an F-89 jet fighter aircraft from Fairchild AFB. The Air Force sent airplanes to several cities to pick up Mountain Rescue members and transport them to the search base. A C-47 landed at the Yakima airport to pick up the CWMR members: Jim Linse, Hal Foss, and me from Yakima. Jack Owens and Jess Peck of Wenatchee were picked up en route, and all were flown to Oroville, WA, where a truck was waiting to transport us to the ranger station in Loomis, WA. At Loomis, search headquarters was set up and planning was underway. Since sleeping space was limited in the ranger station, the CWMR members put their sleeping bags on the floor and got a few hours of sleep under

the tables while the operation leaders organized the search areas for each team.

Mountain Rescue members from all over the state participated. Some of the Seattle MRC members found the first crewman who had ejected. He had landed by parachute near where the plane crashed. He survived and was picked up by a Canadian helicopter and flown to a hospital in Canada.

Hal Foss, Lynn Buchanan, and Jim Linse of CWMR checking a map before leaving the National Guard pickup and starting on a search up one of the many creek valleys around Loomis. USAF photo.

An interesting sidelight to that mission occurred when the local Sheriff arrived on the scene of the crash by horseback after the Canadian helicopter left with the USAF pilot, and while the medic from Canada was awaiting its return. In those days helicopters were very weight restricted, and the pilots of the rescue helicopter had to leave their crewman behind when they flew the USAF crewman to the hospital in Canada. The Sheriff asked who the fellow was that was standing there in the dark. When told that he was a Canadian, the Sheriff said he was going to arrest him for crossing the border illegally. Just when things were getting rather heated, the Canadian helicopter returned. The pilot lowered the hoist cable, illuminated by the big landing light on the bottom of the bird, the crewman snapped on to the hook and disappeared up into the night!

After several days of futile searching in the snow-covered terrain for the missing man, the Mountain Rescue members were flown back to their respective cities and the search was terminated. It was nineteen years later that a hunter found the ejection seat and some human bones in a densely forested area. The crewman had never separated from his ejection seat and had been buried in the snow where he landed.

In those days (1963), Mountain Rescue Teams were using the Motorola "lunchbox" radios. They were much smaller than earlier models, which weighed about ten pounds and had long antennas, but the new ones still weighed about five pounds. The smaller size, similar to a metal lunchbox, was really appreciated, but these smaller radios were still "line of sight," as were the larger and older ones still using the MRA frequency of 155.160. However, once the teams got into some of the narrow, steep-walled canyons around the Loomis area, they were almost totally useless (but five pounds instead of ten pounds of uselessness).

Late at night on 15 September 1968, a call came to the Yakima County Sheriff's Office (YSO) that two severely hypothermic hikers were in their sleeping bags, no tent, along the Cascade Crest Trail in the Goat Rocks. The remaining three members of the party had found the tent of a solo hiker in McCall Basin and asked him to pass the word. The solo hiker had put the very cold, but still moving, hikers into his tent and started the hike out in the dark, back down the trail to the west side of White Pass. When he reached his car, he drove to a telephone and called YSO with the message. CWMR was alerted and planned on going in at first light from the trailhead behind and up the road from Clear Lake. YSO also arranged for several packhorses and a handler to follow CWMR in and bring out the hikers and their gear. (See the newspaper article "From the Top" printed earlier.)

Lex Maxwell, Dave Mahre, and I led the first CWMR team up the trail. The team included: Judy Beehler, Bob Crain, Jim Carlson, Dallas Hake, Jim Linse, John Thompson Jr., and Dorothy Wood. When we reached the Crest Trail, we continued to the top of the ridge south of McCall Basin. There we split, with three of us continuing south and the rest of the first team returning to McCall Basin to help the following team get those hikers ready to return to the highway. They stayed in the Basin to attend to the fellows who had walked out to that point.

The west wind was blowing across the crest of the ridge so hard that we could lean against it with our bodies at almost sixty degrees to the horizontal. After quite a struggle south along the ridge, the two hikers and their sleeping bags were spotted in a shallow declivity just east of the trail with their packs standing next to them. When the five hikers realized that they were unable to continue walking in the storm, one of them, Ding Cannon, helped the lady into her sleeping bag and crawled into his to try to rest until the rest of the members of their party got help for them. Ding's sleeping bag had almost eight inches of snow covering it with just a small hole where the warm air exhaled by him had melted it.

At some point the hypothermic lady had crawled more than halfway out of her sleeping bag and removed her coat while lying there in the snow. She had died, probably of hypothermia.

Ding was unconscious in his sleeping bag, but we were able to awaken him. We walked him out, with two of us taking turns walking alongside him and holding him up for the several miles out to the campsite in McCall Basin. At the campsite, the horse party was waiting, so Ding was placed in two sleeping bags, one on each leg and with the upper part of the bags wrapped around his body, one bag on each side. I led the horse down the trail in the dark with Beehler walking ahead to look out for low branches or partially down tree trunks that Cannon might collide with in his lethargic state.

Part way down, Beehler was standing by the trail in the gathering darkness. When I asked why she was there, she pointed out some tree trunks that were making a moaning sound as they rubbed against each other in the darkness just ahead. It sounded so spooky that she decided to stay closer to Ding, the horse, and me to keep her company. The horse was impatient to get back to the barn for the night and was often stepping on my heels as we went downhill on the trail. It was hard to tell which of us was happiest when we got to the ambulance waiting at the trailhead and loaded Ding aboard. The rest of the CWMR party and the horsemen brought out Cannon's gear and escorted the three members of his party out with them. The deceased lady was brought out by a packhorse when the weather improved a few days later.

On 11 January 1972, a massive search began in Pend Oreille County for two Spokane hunters who had disappeared while elk hunting near the Canadian border. The weather was generally nasty with rain and snow each day. Each of the Washington State Mountain Rescue Teams sent members up for a few days of the weeklong search. In addition, teams from the US Army, US Air Force and Civil Air Patrol searched through the cold, wet, brushy forest with no luck. Seattle MRC was providing the base leadership for the search parties, marking their routes on a map and then checking with each party as they returned to mark the area they had covered. Seattle MRC assigned me as base Operations

Leader (OL) for the search on one day. I had to direct more than 100 searchers in the field in many teams. When each team got back at the end of the day, I had to record the area they had searched on our base map. After the search was officially terminated, some family members found the bodies of the hunters well outside the area MRC was told they had been hunting.

In March of 1975, Douglas Buchanan and Jim Carlson were attempting the climb of a peak in the Central Alaska Range (McGinnis Peak). (See "AVALANCHE," page xxvii) A massive ice avalanche fell from a hanging glacier on an adjacent ridge and dropped about a half mile down the mountain and across the glacier the two climbers were ascending. Both climbers made a dash to get behind a large serac near the tent. Douglas got there but was buried to his armpits. Jim was buried beside the tent. After Douglas dug himself out of the frozen snow and ice chunks with his hard hat, he looked for any sign of Jim but couldn't find where he was. Douglas found one ski and hiked out, making one ski track and one boot track. Later, on our trip out after finding Jim's body, we followed the same route and found that a pack of wolves had been following Douglas's track, probably thinking they had dinner somewhere ahead. Doug said his walking had been rather erratic, probably giving them the idea.

I was called in the middle of the night in Yakima and asked to go to the scene and help recover the body from the avalanche. Douglas, another climber, and I went on the mission and were flown to the scene by an Alaska State Patrol trooper in one of their helicopters. We then spent several days in the range in winter conditions similar to my Arctic trip three years later. We found the body, buried seven feet deep, dug it out, and marked its location for later helicopter extraction.

Flying into the Alaska Range in March 1975. The avalanche was around the corner to the right on the upper part of the glacier.

Douglas Buchanan (with skis and orange gaiters) on the hike out of the Alaska Range during the blizzard.

We hiked out from the scene in blizzard conditions. When we had a braided river to cross, there was a bit of discussion—wear snowshoes or not? After trying the snowshoes, it was discovered that the ice was too thin to hold them up and it was easier to wade the stream with our boots on. With snowshoes on, when we broke through, it was really difficult to remove the snowshoes from the rushing water through the hole they made in the ice! The water of the stream was about knee-deep and rather cold! When we got to the highway, we hitched a ride in a pickup back to Fairbanks.

Fall of 1976.

In the photo of Mt. St. Helens above, Dogs Head is the rock ridge just left of the centerline. Forsythe Glacier descends from the summit directly toward the viewer. The usual climbing route was up the right side of Dogs Head (up the snow finger in the shadow) then a long diagonal to the left and just over the left skyline to the crater rim out of sight to the right. The long rock ridge visible in the shadow to the right near the summit is "The Boot" on the "Lizard" route.

Just after 2100 on 27 April 1975, I was called by Seattle MRC to assist in a night mission on Mt. St. Helens where several college students were buried in an avalanche on Forsythe Glacier. Seattle called me because of my extensive avalanche search training. Immediately, I called the state patrol to find if the highway was being patrolled that late in the evening—it was not. (The trooper's comment: "Don't do anything stupid!")

Probe line on St. Helens. Note the orange-and-blue "MRC Uniform" rain parkas. These were manufactured and tried out for a couple of years, but did not meet with universal approval!

I then drove my Karman Ghia over White Pass, maybe a little faster than usual, to get there at the start of the search. At the parking lot, I changed from my street clothes into long johns and climbing gear. The wind was blowing hard, and the snow was really coming down. Visibility was down to a couple of hundred yards. While I was pulling on my fishnet underwear standing beside the Ghia, I felt every flake! The Seattle and Tacoma teams were arriving at the parking lot on the north side of Mt. St. Helens when I got there at 2300 that night. (That parking lot was buried in the eruption of Mt. St. Helens in 1980.)

Shortly after we got on the mountain, Paul Williams and I cancelled the search because of the continuing heavy snowstorm, high wind, and the very real danger of another avalanche catching the Mountain Rescue teams. The storm met all the criteria listed as precursors of another avalanche. We all went back home to wait for the storm to abate. The students had been buried for many hours by that time, so there was no chance they would have survived.

Looking up Forsyth Glacier. Dogs Head to the left. There are two recent avalanche termini to the left. They both crossed what would have been our route to the avalanche scene! The campsite is on the flat above the probe line.

When we returned on the morning of the 29th to do the body search, we found that a massive avalanche had come down on the route we had been following that night. If we had continued up the mountain that night, we would have been caught in that avalanche.

On scene that morning, we formed several probe lines, but shortly after the start of the probing near where we thought the campsite was, one team found a tent. After digging out the tents, we found the bodies of the students still in their sleeping bags. They had been buried under six to seven feet of heavy snow as they slept and died of suffocation without being able to move.

Moving the bodies off Forsythe Glacier. The teams were moving across the top of the avalanche. The LZ was in the gap in the ridge at the top left of the picture ("The Sugar Bowl").

On 8 February 1976, two climbers fell as they were leaving the crater rim on their descent of Mt. St. Helens (9,677 feet elevation then). They were part of a group that had climbed the mountain together. Once they had reached the summit where the old collapsed fire lookout sat on the west rim of the crater, they had returned across the crater to begin the descent down the very steep slope to Dogs Head (the rock outcrop that juts out on the east side where Forsyth Glacier used to be). The glacier surface and all the exposed rocks were covered with a quarter

of an inch or more of clear ice from a freezing rain a day or so earlier. In those days, before the 1980 eruption of St. Helens, the usual climb went from a parking lot at the northeast base of the mountain, up to the top of Dogs Head, then a long diagonal climb across the glaciers to the east side of the crater rim. From the rim, the route led almost straight west across the shallow crater filled with ice and snow. The descent followed the same route back down to the parking lot.

Winter photo of Mt. St. Helens circa 1976 from just west of the parking lot. The route went from the left foreground to the top of Dogs Head, the big rock bluff on the left, then to the summit crater rim just beyond the high point on the left. The summit is out of sight on the far side of the crater rim. Forsythe Glacier descends from this side of the crater rim to the foreground, right of Dogs Head.

Others of the party who had seen the start of the fall stated that one climber had fallen after making just a few steps down the steep slope outside the crater. The rope partner was not prepared for a belay because they had just stepped onto the steep ice from the crater rim to descend along the Dogs Head route. The fall was so sudden and they went so fast down the glacier that they were out of sight almost immediately.

Both climbers were wearing crampons, carried ice axes, and were roped together. They had some experience, but they had not been climbing for very long. When last seen by other climbers, they were literally tumbling and bouncing down the glacier surface. They had gone out of sight and the other climbers did not feel they could safely follow them, so they descended and called Mountain Rescue.

Mt. St. Helens crater from the summit in 1976. Two climbers are approaching the summit after crossing the snow-filled crater. The pointed rock on the east crater rim is visible in the last photo and is where the route comes over the east edge of the crater.

Both Seattle Mountain Rescue Council (MRC) and Tacoma Mountain Rescue (TMRU) were called for the mission. It was going to be a long night mission searching the east side of Mt. St.

Helens for the fallen climbers. There was not much hope, but if either of them were alive, they needed care as soon as possible. George Sainsbury of MRC called me late in the evening and asked me to assist Seattle Mountain Rescue on the search because of my glacier climbing experience.

It was even later when all of us got to the mountain. As members of MRC and TMRU arrived at the road end, we were sent out in teams of two or three roped together and assigned an approximate elevation to search going south across the glaciers. I was paired up with a Seattle MRC member. We started up from the parking lot, which was located where the road ended just a bit northeast of the lower end of Forsythe Glacier in those days. The rope teams climbed to the top of Dogs Head, then when they reached their assigned elevation, they went south around the mountain looking for any sign of the climbers. It was already night, but there was a nearly full moon. We had been assured that a US Coast Guard helicopter equipped with a "Night Sun" light would be arriving very shortly to assist us in the search by lighting up any areas where we needed light.

This was in the days before mountain climbing was as popular as it is now, so most of us had hand-forged crampons from Switzerland or Austria. The points were square and about an inch and a half long. Serious climbers often filed the points very sharp for steep ice climbing. My partner was a bit unhappy about crossing the rock ridges between the glaciers and snowfields because he had just sharpened his crampons and didn't want to dull them on the rocks. The answer was to take them off, cross the rocks, then put them back on. However, with the hard, slick glaze of clear ice on the surface of the rocks, we both felt much safer wearing them right across the rock.

When the Coast Guard helicopter got there, the "Night Sun" description really fit the light. It was so bright that we could have read a newspaper when the helicopter went over our heads. The problem was that after he flew over, we had lost our night vision and were relatively blind in the bright moonlight until our eyes adapted again. An additional problem was communication. If we needed a place lighted, we could call the MRC truck sitting in the parking lot on our VHF radio. They would then call the King County Sheriff's office (MRC base station) on the truck radio. The sheriff's office would relay the message via a long-distance telephone call to the Coast Guard station in Astoria, Oregon. The Coast Guard station would radio the message to the helicopter. Of course, by the time the message got to it, the helicopter had moved a couple of miles. The series of steps necessary made the response to our requests difficult.

My partner and I reached the fall line position below where the two climbers had slipped and fallen. We could see equipment and blood smears on some of the rocks where they had hit and bounced. The mountain has curving rock ridges that swing to the north as they descend the mountain, but the climbers had fallen relatively straight down, bouncing over the rock ridges and continuing on to the next glacier. We followed the fall line and were joined by other rope teams going down the mountain. The fall had been much longer than anyone had expected. The layer of smooth clear ice on the surface had probably extended the distance of the fall considerably.

At about the lower midpoint of the snow peak (7,000 to 8,000 feet) on Ape Glacier, we came upon the bodies where they had been stopped by impact with a rock ridge. Both climbers were deceased and had severe crush injuries. Many facial and head injuries were sustained in the fall to the point that it was hard to tell which body belonged to which name. It was speculated that the crampons had exacerbated the original injuries by causing leg fractures in the first attempts to stop. Once the fall was developed, there was no way to stop since they were both bouncing and cartwheeling through the air.

It was early daylight by the time we located the bodies. We radioed for a team to bring two body bags and litters from the parking lot to our location. We had time to sit on the rocks and rest a bit until a team arrived with the equipment after travelling almost a quarter of the way around the mountain. The rest of the search teams had arrived at our location by then, so we had enough manpower to lower the litters down and around the mountain carefully, with several carries across the low rock ridges between the glaciers and snowfields. The clear ice surface really slowed down the recovery as well, since we all had to be very careful of our footing as we worked. After the all-night search, everyone was tired, and we didn't need any injuries on the return to base. It was midmorning by the time we returned to the vehicles. Then came the long drive back to our homes, Seattle and Yakima being about equidistant from Mt. St. Helens.

For myself, I put 366 miles on my personal vehicle and seventeen and a half hours of time spent on the mission, a fairly long day in itself after a normal workday the previous day in Yakima.

I was called for another MRC mission to Mt. St. Helens in November of 1976 to search for two climbers from Portland who had disappeared. This mission involved teams searching on foot, as well as a couple of Oregon National Guard UH-1N (Huey) helicopters searching from the air. On the first day of searching (9 November 1976), all the teams searched up the mountain, climbing to the summit by various routes, then we were picked up on the summit by helicopters and carried down to the parking lot. No one found any trace of the climbers that day, and we all returned home. The helicopters continued the search from the air for the climbers.

Late on the third day of aerial searching, a helicopter crew spotted the climbers' rope. It was hanging from the lower lip of a crevasse. The crevasse was high on the Forsythe Glacier where the climbers had fallen into it. Two US Air Force Pararescue fellows (PJs) were lowered from the helicopter into the crevasse, where they had seen the climbers' rope. The PJs determined the climbers were dead but while they were in the crevasse, the helicopter went back to Portland to refuel. As soon as the noise of the helicopter disappeared, the PJs could hear the glacier ice creaking and groaning as it moved. Mountain climbers would not have been that concerned, but the PJs wanted out, NOW! By the time the helicopter had refueled and returned, the PJs were rather upset.

That was three and a half years before the eruption of Mt. St. Helens, and in retrospect, one wonders how much of the noise may have been from the shifting of rocks below the mountain. They were right over the spot where the eruption occurred in 1980.

I was called that night by Seattle MRC to return to Mt. St. Helens in the morning (12 November 1976). I was there early with MRC and Tacoma (TMRU) at the parking lot below the glacier when the Operations Leaders (George Sainsbury and John Simac) picked those of us who would go high on the mountain. We were flown to a landing zone (LZ) high on the Forsythe and climbed from there to the scene of the accident.

The upper section of Forsythe had several vertical pitches, requiring ice screws to lower the body bags over the cliffs. It was there they found how flimsy the old military surplus body bags were. The one they were using for the second body started to tear apart while the body was being lowered over an ice cliff. I was lowered over the cliff on a separate rope to secure the body with turns of rope tied around it to keep the bag from coming completely apart. The recovery of the two bodies took all day. After we got the second body to the bottom of the cliff and were taking it down to the top of Dogs Head, we were notified that the Huey would stop flying when it got dark, so we had to hurry. The body and some of the team were picked up in the last few minutes before darkness stopped all flying for the day. The Huey

landed in the parking lot lighted by the headlights of several vehicles. The rest of the Mountain Rescue folks and I hiked down in
the darkness from Dogs Head.

*The east side of Mt. Rainier from Sourdough Pass. Emmons
Glacier is in the center. Steamboat Prow is the rocky triangle on
the right side of the photo with Interglacier flowing down in the
middle of the triangle to the valley in the lower right corner of
the photo. Photo from 13 July 2002.*

In December 1976, three mountain climbers made a climb of
Mt. Rainier via Liberty Ridge. A storm moved in and the climbers
did not return to their homes at the time they had planned. Their
planned route of descent was to go down the mountain to the
east, toward the White River access to Mt. Rainier National Park
(MRNP). With the weather as bad as it was, there was no way rescuers could go looking for them in the storm, but as soon as the
storm went away, Seattle, Tacoma, and Olympic mountain rescue
units were called in to see if they could find where the climbers
were. (See the editorial "Rainier Rescuers Respond" at the beginning of the book.)

I was called by Al Errington of Seattle MRC on 8 December 1976 at 1615 hours to see if I could join them in the morning at the White River entrance to the park. I agreed to go and started packing my climbing gear for the trip over the pass. At that time it was snowing one inch per hour at Paradise Ranger Station on the south side of the mountain. An Army pilot, Warrant Officer Cleves, had a Huey helicopter on the ground near the north entrance of the park and reported it was icing up while sitting there. After most of my packing was done, I got a bit of sleep and arose at 0300 to finish it. At 0400 I was on my way to the park via Chinook Pass. It was snowing on the pass, chains required, but I made it to the White River entrance fairly fast. We were diverted to the Ranger Creek airport northeast of the park where the Army provided a Huey helicopter to transport the Mountain Rescue folks as high on the mountain as possible.

A team of us from Seattle MRC loaded into the Huey and rode to a landing zone on Interglacier near the south side of Steamboat Prow and below Mt. Ruth, an 8,700-foot peak on the south ridge, where we would be able to look over a portion of the east side of Mt. Rainier. As the helicopter turned north to go over the steep south wall of Steamboat Prow, we were caught in some very severe turbulence. We were all securely belted in, but the wind shook the helicopter, and therefore us, like a dog shaking a bone! That was one of the few times I have experienced severe turbulence. (Severe turbulence is defined by the Federal Aviation Administration [FAA] as "when the control of the aircraft is in doubt.") The pilot recovered, then hovered over a flat spot high on Interglacier and dropped us off. It took us three hours to climb from there to the top of Mt. Ruth to look down on the Emmons Glacier.

When we reached the top of Mt. Ruth at 1500 hours, the climbers were spotted at about 11,000 feet on the Winthrop Glacier on their way down Mt. Rainier. We called in and returned down Mt. Ruth to the LZ to be picked up. A helicopter picked up the climbers and took them to the Ranger Creek airport, where a doctor there examined them and declared they were in good shape after their unplanned campout in the storm. When a helicopter came to pick us up, we met a different crew that flew us back to the airport we had left earlier in the day. There the previous crew showed us a quarter-inch high, very sharp wrinkle halfway around the tail rotor housing. The whole tail of the aircraft had been severely bent in the turbulence. The aircraft was "red tagged" and was waiting for a semitrailer to be brought in to haul it back to Ft. Lewis.

The pilot then explained that the turbulence we had encountered was what the FAA called "extreme," where the aircraft itself was damaged by the turbulence. We were lucky!

There were quite a few other missions where I was called individually to participate as a member of Seattle MRC because of my specialized training, including one mission to Mt. Baker on 8 September 1977 for a helicopter with a two-man crew that had disappeared the day before. The mountain was involved in a major storm. It was a long drive, but when I got to base camp in the town of Glacier (WA), a C-130 was flying over the mountain listening to the helicopter ELT. Through a hole in the storm clouds, the C-130 crew saw the helicopter sitting on the summit with two persons waving to them. When the weather improved, another helicopter went to the top of the mountain and retrieved the crew, then they flew in some fresh batteries, started the stranded bird, and flew it away. A Mountain Rescue team from Seattle had started climbing to the summit before this happened, so they were recalled. The rest of the folks who were gathering for a rescue were released, and all the foot troops started back home, relieved that we did not have to make the climb of Mt. Baker in the storm!

It was determined later that the pilot of the helicopter had landed on the summit of Mt. Baker the afternoon before the storm to do some sightseeing on his way back from a job near there and had shut down the engine. When the aircraft would not start after they returned, they could not radio their predicament because they had run down the batteries.

As a bit of background, during my fifty-eight years in Mountain Rescue, I worked with the Crag Rats of Hood River on several Mt. Hood missions, and they worked with us on Mt. Adams. Then the Department of Emergency Services of Washington State started telling us not to respond to Oregon since Oregon didn't have the protections that Washington had for us if we got hurt on a rescue. However, when a mission is called in the mountains, most of us will respond, regardless of what the bureaucrats in Olympia (WA) say. I have been on Mt. Hood several times in response to a call for help, whether to the south side, the north side, or even once to the northwest corner.

I have been to the top of Mt. Hood thirteen times by both north side and south side routes, so I was comfortable with calls to go to the assistance of someone in trouble on the mountain.

On 22 May 1977, I had an adventure on the south side of Mt. Hood when I climbed the mountain by myself (NOT recommended, but I have done it). With all the climbers who usually climb that route on a weekend, a solo climb is rather a misnomer. How can one be solo with forty or fifty other climbers on the same route at nearly the same time? I have had several adventures on this route, but that climb was going to be a day to tell about for quite a while.

South side of Mt. Hood from above Timberline Lodge. Crater Rock is the stone pinnacle just to the left of center in front of the crater wall. Hogback is the snow ridge in the center with the bergschrund (a big crevasse) across it near the top. After crossing the schrund, the route swings right into a snow-filled gully. Photo from 25 June 2009.

Before daylight in the morning, I left my vehicle and hiked up the mountain to the Silcox Hut. The snow was frozen hard, so I had my crampons on right from the start. I had a bite to eat from my pack at Silcox and continued on paralleling the chairlift. By the time I got to Crater Rock (the big rock pillar to the left of the route) and climbed to the "Hogback" (a ridge of snow carved by the wind between Crater Rock and the steep wall of the old crater), the sun had come up.

The climb was going well, the weather was great, and I was passing most of the other climbers, many of whom were not as well acclimated to the altitude as I was that early in the summer. The snow up that part of the climb was getting softer, so I had taken my crampons off on the Hogback and was kicking my own set of steps parallel to a Mazama party. I wanted to be ahead of them on the steep part of the climb. A large party on a steep climb can be much slower than a single individual.

On the Hogback, I went around the end of the bergschrund and was catching up with and passing the Mazamas on their climb of the mountain. For many of them, it was the first time on such a steep snow climb as it is there on Mt. Hood above the schrund. They were roped together, five or six on a rope, carefully putting their feet into the footsteps kicked into the snow by their leader. Each one was carrying a coil of the slack rope between themselves and the next climber and each one so close to the climber ahead that they were almost touching them. When I reached the point where the route went through a gully and narrowed down to only eight to ten feet wide, a grapefruit-sized chunk of ice came whizzing down from above and struck the midpoint of my right thigh! It knocked me over backward and I tumbled down the steep slope. As I fell head over heels a couple of hundred feet down the slope, I managed to flatten out and get into a self-arrest position to stop myself. I was below the gully and about twenty feet away from the long line of climbers. No one was looking at me. Apparently they were so shocked by the sight of someone falling past them that they were almost frozen in position, moving their feet like robots.

I was pretty sure my femur was broken because of the pain. The Mazamas were ignoring me, and I was concentrating on whether I would be able to move my leg. After a few minutes, I realized the bone must have been intact and determined there was no serious injury. I carefully cut a step in the steep snow and climbed back to my feet. There was no comment from the beginning climbers. When I was sure that I could still support myself on that leg, and that I could move it, I looked at the line of beginners and asked if I could move into their line of steps. I think most of them were too scared by the angle of snow they were climbing to even look at me, but eventually one of the rope leaders climbed to where he was even with me and told me I could get in front of his rope if I still wanted to continue up.

After I was in the line and using the footsteps, he asked what had happened, then said that my fall had been rather spectacular; he thought I was going all the way to the crater bottom!

At that point we were only a few hundred feet below the summit, so it was just one slow step at a time to the summit. Once there, I looked at the spectacularly clear weather, probably signed the register, maybe not, then started down. For a while, I just carefully backed down the steps the Mazamas had made, moving one foot at a time. As I got closer to the bergschrund, I turned around and started plunging my heels into the softer snow and making a bit more speed, but still moving slowly and carefully. I reached the hogback and continued down in still softer snow, but I could tell a hematoma (a large accumulation of blood in the muscles below the skin) was growing at the point of impact on my thigh.

As I was descending around the base of Crater Rock, I saw several climbers looking down the almost vertical snow slope dropping to the White River Glacier, so I went over to join them. They were looking at a climber who had fallen to the bottom of the snow-filled valley. They said the climber's two partners had already run down toward the lodge to get help. At that point, the drop into the canyon of the glacier was almost vertical, and no one was willing to go down to help the fellow. I asked if someone had a rope and one did. The two of us tied in and walked down the mountain a couple of hundred feet, then went over the side of the canyon where it was not quite as steep and made our way to the injured fellow. After assessing his injuries, which consisted of a broken leg and multiple bruises, we improvised a splint from a couple of ice axes, then made a litter of sorts from the climbing rope. We maneuvered between the crevasses very carefully down the glacier until the slope was not as steep and there was not as much distance from the top of the glacier up to the top of the south slope of Mt. Hood. There, we climbed out onto the skiing areas while sliding the injured fellow on the snow.

Photo showing the scene of the 22 May 1977 accident. The climber fell down the steep snow slope just left of the center of the photo into the bottom of the White River Glacier canyon. We carried him in the bottom of the canyon to the more gradual exit from the canyon bottom over the bench in the lower left corner of the photo. Photo from 8 January 2012.

When the climbers had reached the lodge and asked for assistance, the lodge folks called Dr. Bangs from Oregon City. Dr. Bangs called for a National Guard helicopter (a Huey), then he and a couple of fellows (one of whom was his son) rode to the mountain in it.

I had a fifteen-minute highway fusee (a red flare) in my pack, so when I had the Huey in sight, I lit it. The helicopter went by us between thirty and forty feet above the surface of the snow and a bit downhill from us. It wove around, searching all over while I stood there on the ski slope waving the fusee! The Huey continued over to the glacier, then slowly flew up to its upper end, circled around for a while, then flew down to the lodge. Apparently someone there told the pilot about the small group of climbers laboring down the mountain, possibly carrying a litter or something, so the Huey flew up to us and landed. Dr. Bangs, who was well known to the Mountain Rescue folks in the area, and the crew chief of the bird came over with a Stokes litter. They assessed the patient, put a better splint on him, placed the patient into the Stokes litter with some blankets, and then flew away to the hospital. We, in our party, thanked each other, and the other climbers strode off down the mountain.

Aerial photo of the summit area of Mt. Hood from the southeast later in the year. The Hogback is the snow ridge between Crater Rock (on the left) and the summit. It is caused by wind blowing around Crater Rock and up the crater wall, leaving a sharp crest on the accumulated snow. The route to the summit follows the top of the Hogback into what, earlier in the summer, is a narrow, snow-filled gully that leads up through the rocks to the summit. In the lower left of the photo is the near vertical wall of snow the climber fell down. There was snow at the bottom of the snow wall at the time of the accident (see page 84). Photo from 12 August 2007.

By then, my thigh was really getting painful, so I was moving much more slowly. I soon saw a Snowcat coming down the mountain and flagged it down. The driver asked what I wanted, and I told him of my injury and asked if I could have a ride to the lodge. He said to hop aboard! I did and rode down to where I could get to my car and drive home. By this time the hematoma on my thigh was about the size of half a grapefruit and was getting really painful. At home, I visited a doctor who told me I should have put an ice (or snow) pack on it and rested, instead of climbing up, down, and rescuing someone else! In a couple of days, I had a Technicolor leg, but it did heal.

One Monday morning (8 May 1978), I received a phone call from a businessman I knew here in Yakima. He told me how his son and three other fellows had been climbing a ridge on Mt. Hood to the west of Glisan Glacier on Sunday. They were pretty close to the top and had to go around a rock gendarme on the ridge. They opted to go around on the snow at the east side of the gendarme and as they got to about the middle of its base, the snow avalanched down the mountain, carrying all four of them down. The slope was extremely steep, and they were tumbling totally out of control right from the start. Quite a wide bergschrund interrupted the snow slope below them, but they were going so fast at that point that they flew across it and continued down the mountain for what appeared to be more than a couple of thousand feet. At the bottom of that section of Mt. Hood, the slope became gentler and they stopped on a relatively flat spot.

They gathered themselves together and accumulated what they could find of their gear. Now what? They were all battered and bruised, but no bones were broken. As they were trying to figure out where they were on the mountain and how to get back to civilization, a Huey helicopter arrived. Someone had seen the fall and called for a rescue. The folks on the other end of the phone line had placed a call to the doctor at Oregon City, who had called the National Guard base, and a Huey was dispatched with the doctor and a couple of climbers.

Since the climbing party was on nearly flat snow when they stopped, the Huey had no trouble landing near them. The crew checked the climbers, gathered their equipment, and loaded them aboard the Huey for the trip to the hospital. All four of them were kept overnight after notifying the wives and families where they were and that they would probably be released from the hospital the next morning.

A couple of the wives left immediately for Oregon. The father of one of the climbers waited until morning before he called me. He pointed out that he had felt there was no reason to hurry down during the night. Since the wives had small cars (I think VW sedans), he felt that he could prevail on me to fly down in my Cherokee 6 to Oregon City airport and pick up the remaining two fellows, his son and the one other climber. The weather was clear, so I was happy to leave immediately. The fellows got a ride from the hospital to the airport, where they met me and climbed in for a ride home. They admitted they were pretty stiff and sore and had patches of skin missing where they had bounced on hard ice and snow during the trip down. We flew past the northwest side of Mt. Hood, and they could point out where the slide had started and where they had stopped. It was truly amazing that they had been airborne all the way across the schrund and survived the fall without serious injury!

The ride home in the airplane was much more comfortable than the long ride in a VW would have been, and they were home resting long before their two buddies got home.

❖ ❖ ❖

Late in the evening on 9 May 1979, George Sainsbury of Seattle MRC called me to help in the recovery of the bodies of Willie Unseold and Janie Diepenbrock, buried in an avalanche on Mt. Rainier the previous weekend as they descended through Cadaver Gap with their climbing party. The weather had been stormy with heavy snowfall at the time of the avalanche and for the week following, preventing any meaningful attempts for recovery of the victims. The weather was improving and was anticipated to be clear for the search the next morning.

I drove from Yakima to the Paradise visitor center in Mt. Rainier National Park that night, slept a few hours in the car, and met MRC and TMRU (Tacoma Mountain Rescue Unit) in the morning. About thirty other Mountain Rescue folks from Seattle and Tacoma assembled at the visitor center. The Park Service briefed everyone on the procedure they had planned. The weather on the mountain was clear with calm winds. Because it was a body search, the rescue team was not offered helicopter transport to the scene. Everyone would be hiking up from the parking lot to the scene just below Cadaver Gap. A couple of TMRU members did not want to make the climb to Camp Muir, so they stayed at the base with the Park Service to assist there. Because the avalanche hazard above Camp Muir was unknown, each member of the team was issued a one-kilogram stick of explosive to carry on top of their packs. One member was issued a package of blasting caps. I got into the line at the end, figuring that they would be out of explosives before they ran out of willing pack-horses. However, the Park Service had it figured out pretty well: one package for each person, with the coil of Primacord for the last one, me! Someone pointed out that the Primacord was good for cutting down trees; just a few wraps would do it. I had a coil of many wraps lying against the back of my neck—on top of the pack.

Arrival of the recoilless rifle at Camp Muir. The normal climbing route from Camp Muir followed the snow slope to the top of the ridge on the skyline.

Everyone had snowshoes, but we soon found that the snow was too hard for them to be useful. So we stacked them under some trees along the route going up to Muir. As we got to Camp Muir, some Forest Service folks arrived in a helicopter. The helicopter left and returned with a seventy-five millimeter recoilless rifle and some ammo slung beneath it. The gun was set up on the snow just north of the buildings. Camp Muir at that time had only a large stone climbers' hut and a stone outhouse.

The recoilless rifle gunners laid a couple of sheets of plywood on the snow to keep the gun from settling in as it was fired. They then fired high explosive projectiles into possible avalanche slopes around the area and above where the avalanche had stopped. Two of the following photos show the rifle firing and then the black smoke of an impact. The slide had come down from Cadaver Gap, flowing first east then slightly north before stopping.

Setting up the recoilless rifle.

The location of the bodies was probably somewhere near the avalanche terminus. There had been another avalanche over the one covering the bodies, but it was shallow and we were quite sure it followed the route of the first one. All the slopes proved stable (the snow was frozen hard) so the gunner fired a few rounds into the big icicles hanging from the stone walls of Gibraltar Rock overhanging the scene.

Cadaver Gap is the low spot between the two vertical rock ridges. The snow and ice visible through Cadaver Gap is on Disappointment Cleaver, a rocky ridge on the other side of Ingraham Glacier, which is out of sight from this position on Cowlitz Glacier.

Since the projectiles caused no new slides, the Park Rangers and Mountain Rescue folks left Camp Muir. We climbed up and curved right toward Cadaver Gap. This took us across to the lower end of the avalanche, which had stopped about 500 feet higher than Muir. By the time we were crossing the center snowfield, the heat of the sun was starting to make the snow soft and slushy.

Firing.

*Impact! The black smudges on the snow
are from projectiles previously fired.*

About that time a large explosion occurred back at Camp Muir, where a cloud of smoke boiled into the air. The senior ranger in the party got on the radio to ask what had happened. The ranger at Muir had decided not to carry the explosives back down and exploded half of them. With the snow on the route in the direct sunlight and getting softer by the minute, he was told rather explicitly *not* to detonate any more until everyone left the area.

Seattle Mountain Rescue personnel climbing toward Cadaver Gap on Mt. Rainier. The black smudges on the snow are where the seventy-five millimeter recoilless rifle projectiles have exploded. The purple pack in the foreground is one of a type that MRC had tried to standardize some years before.

The team continued up to the avalanche terminus. The senior ranger assigned duties to the different rangers. The one in charge of the probe line gave directions to the Mountain Rescue folks in metric measurements: "x" centimeters between your feet; "x" centimeters between persons on the line. Everyone was looking at each other with blank looks and amusement. We were volunteers, and metric was not the way we had been trained many years before. The senior ranger called me out of the probe line, then asked the ranger in charge of the probe line to take charge of the shovel crews. He asked me to take charge of the probe line. I organized a coarse probe line using inches for measurements, and we started probing up the avalanche from its toe.

Following the climbing rope from one body to the other.
Second from left: Gary Glenn. Right side: Al Errington.

After only a few probe lines were completed up the hill, we found Willi. We then followed his climbing rope to Janie. We dug the bodies out of the snow and placed them in body bags.

After placing the bodies in rescue sleds, we slid them down to Paradise, where they were loaded into a hearse for the ride to Olympia. As we passed the pile of snowshoes on the way back to Paradise, we each picked up our own pair before checking out with the Park Service at the visitor center.

It was early evening and another mission was over, with a long drive ahead before everyone was safely home.

❖ ❖ ❖

Returning to the Paradise ranger station.

On 2 Oct 1979, a solo climber from Seattle was missing on a climb of Lyman Glacier on Mt. Adams. Seattle MRC arranged with the Army to fly a Chinook with a few Seattle MRC team members to Mt. Adams to search for him. MRC arranged for the helicopter to come by the Yakima airport to pick me up. The climber's body was spotted high on the mountain, and one team of three or four MRC members was lowered by winch for the body recovery.

They brought the body out of the icefall and slid it to a more level place at close to 11,000 feet, where it could be picked up by the Chinook helicopter. The body was winched aboard through the hole in the floor of the bird. When the first MRC team member climbed into the "horse collar" (a loose loop of rope with a canvas covering that is fastened to the end of the cable) and was starting to be winched aboard, the winch on the helicopter jammed the cable, leaving him dangling about fifteen feet below the Chinook.

At that altitude, the slope of the glacier is extremely steep, so not a lot of room was available to maneuver the helicopter for recovery of the team member. A bit of jockeying of the Chinook was necessary before they could descend enough to let the fellow on the winch step out of the horse collar on a flat enough place so he was not in danger of falling down the mountain. He then climbed up to rejoin his teammates.

The team members preferred to leave with the helicopter since they were not equipped for a safe night on the mountain. They also had flown to that high altitude from a much lower altitude (Seattle) without any time or physical effort in the interval. This can contribute to altitude sickness and makes a bivouac less than desirable. The helicopter and the Mountain Rescue members moved to a rather precarious position where the turning helicopter rotor blades were uncomfortably close to the rocks while the climbers got aboard through the side door via the short entry ladder. Doing so consumed additional time and fuel before we could start home.

The pilot decided the best option was to fly to the Yakima Firing Center (now Yakima Training Center) to refuel before going back to the other side of the Cascades. On the way to the Firing Center, he remained at 11,000 feet to give him more room to maneuver if the fuel ran out en route. The "low fuel" warning light illuminated significantly before he reached his destination, but the pilot assured the MRC members that he could auto-rotate to a landing if the bird ran out of fuel. But then again, all aircraft do land one way or another eventually. After landing at the Yakima Firing Center airport, he told the crew that he was down to fumes, which was about a hundred pounds of fuel, with just a few minutes of flying left to go.

The body and I were both left at the Firing Center to be retrieved by the Yakima County Coroner. I hitched a ride with him from the Firing Center back to my car at the Yakima airport.

In a search on 21 Sep 1980, CWMR and Yakima SAR were called out by YSO very late in the afternoon to see if they could locate some "elderly" ladies who had gone hiking for a couple of days on the Pacific Crest Trail and had not returned. Both of our teams went up the road west of Bumping Lake and were sent up different trails. By the time we left the cars and started hiking up the trail, it was well after dark. The SAR folks started up one trail and CWMR another toward Fish Lake. It was assumed that the ladies would be coming down the trail the SAR folks were on, so the search for them should have been easy.

When CWMR was about a mile up the trail we were to follow, we were walking beside a noisy stream for a short distance. We could still hear the SAR folks talking as they were enthusiastically going up their trail in the distance. At that point a small campfire was burning across the stream that should have been visible from each trail. We shouted to see if the folks at the campfire could hear us. They could. In fact, it was a lady that answered. After shouting back and forth a few times, we decided to wade the stream, cross the intervening swamp, and check on that party. We discovered that the ladies at the campfire were indeed the ones that both teams were looking for.

The ladies were less than a mile from the road, but when they had reached that point, it was getting dark. With the swampy area ahead and the stream audible in the distance, they decided to move off the trail into a good camping spot for the night then go back to the trail in the morning to finish their hike. They were a well-prepared hiking party and had everything they needed for another night out.

It was shorter for them to go out on the trail CWMR had been following and since we were there, we assisted the ladies to break camp and helped them across the swamp and the stream. Base was notified by radio and the SAR team was recalled. A short time later, SAR and the CWMR team were back at the cars, accompanied by the "lost ladies." Another successful mission was accomplished. (The ladies did not feel they were "lost," nor were they any older than some of the CWMR folks.)

On 29 Sep 1995, we had another mission, where Central Washington Mountain Rescue (CWMR) was asked by the Crag Rats to assist on a search of the northwest side of Mt. Hood. Several of us from CWMR drove down that afternoon and spent the night at the road end. We joined the Crag Rats on the mountain at daylight and each team was assigned an area to search. Four of us from CWMR were searching across Sandy Glacier, a long hike across and back to the moraine, looking into crevasses and across the broken top of the glacier. When we got back to the moraine, we took a break for lunch. Joe Roemer, one of our CWMR members, put his hand on a large boulder for balance while climbing off the glacier.

The boulder rolled, not far, but enough to catch Joe's hand between it and an adjacent boulder before stopping. The injury to Joe's hand was extremely painful, possibly with a broken bone. We pried the rocks apart to free his hand then walked with him to meet a couple of Crag Rats, who escorted Joe to their vehicle and took him to a doctor. The rest of us continued the search until I was radioed to come and pick up Joe. He had ridden to Mt. Hood with me, and they asked me to take him back home. He had a crush injury to his hand and was really impressed with the care he had received, but was glad to be on his way home. He was one handed for a few weeks but recovered fully. In spite of the warnings from Olympia, we found the medical care in Oregon for our team member couldn't have been better or more prompt.

On 16 September 1999, I was called by the Yakima Sheriff's Office and asked if I could guide an Army helicopter to a location on the MJB Trail "somewhere north of the Tieton ranger station." The folks on duty at the Sheriff's office that day did not know where that trail was, and those who would know were not available. All they knew was that the injured person was on the MJB Trail. I had hiked that trail several times, so I was happy to go along. An injured horseman down in the valley needed to be transported out to the hospital. I joined the helicopter (an Army UH-60 Blackhawk) at the airport and directed the pilot to the beginning of the trail high on the ridge above Rimrock Lake. Once we were down in the valley north of the ridge, we could make radio contact with the horse group and were directed to the location of the patient. The valley is heavily timbered, so the helicopter could not go to the exact location. The UH-60 hovered ten to fifteen feet above the treetops over a small clearing, then lowered the medic with a Stokes litter on the hoist cable to the ground. The medic and some of the horsemen hiked to the location of the injured fellow, treated him, secured him into the Stokes, and then carried him back to the clearing below the hovering helicopter.

While this was happening on the ground, the pilot would periodically call to get an update on the progress from the medic and tell him the fuel status of the helicopter. The amount of fuel remaining in the helicopter was getting rather critical when the patient was finally hooked on to the cable and hoisted into the helicopter. As the crew chief was helping bring the medic and the patient into the bird, the pilot turned and headed to Yakima, climbing all the way. He stayed high until he was over the Yakima airport, then made his descent, explaining that if the engine quit from fuel starvation, he would be able to auto-rotate to the ground, preferably at the airport. The engine kept running until he was on the ground and could do the customary post-flight procedures. He then dropped me off at the airport, fueled up, flew the patient to the hospital, and returned to the Firing Center. Another successful mission, but with three hours and twenty minutes of flight time!

On 8 October 2007, my wife, Connie Buchanan, and I were called for a search for a Cessna Grand Caravan (Cessna 208) on a mountainside west of Yakima, near Rimrock Lake. CWMR, Tacoma MR (TMRU), Olympic MR, and Seattle MRC (SMR) were all called in the evening after the plane was reported missing and a hunter had called the Yakima Sheriff's Office saying he had heard an airplane crash on the ridge north of his location. The next day an air search was conducted with all of us standing around, as everyone expected the airplanes to be able to find it rather rapidly. The Grand Caravan was a large airplane. The air search was unsuccessful, so late in the afternoon several teams were sent up the very steep mountainside where the hunter had heard the crash. As it got dark, most of the folks not on those teams settled in for the night in their sleeping bags or went back to Yakima. The first positive clue came when one of the ground teams climbing the mountainside reported smelling fuel, then they traversed upwind to the site of the crash. Since it was well after dark by then, the ground teams returned to the base area to spend the night and plan for the next day's operation.

The next day, Fran Sharp, TMRU, was in charge of selecting personnel to return to the crash site. She selected TMRU members and both of us Buchanans to be in the first team to cordon off the crash site and start recovering body parts and putting them in bags. The TMRU members had Kevlar suits and rubber gloves issued to them and were the ones assigned inside the taped-off crash scene area. The two of us were assigned to search the ground just outside the taped-off area to look for any more body parts. Only a few pieces were found outside the approximately 100-foot diameter circle of yellow tape.

The first view of the aircraft. It was more than forty feet long and collapsed to a length of about twelve feet. It came almost straight down, so vertical that it only broke one tree and tipped another over. The red color is on the bottom of the empennage. Off to the right is one of the wings. The other is behind the trees to the left of the picture, shattered and turned inside out.

The rest of the Mountain Rescue folks carried tools and supplies up to the scene and were available to help carry body bags to the small clearing, where they could be hoisted up to the helicopter when the King County UH-1 arrived. It arrived about midmorning, lowered a crewman on its hoist, then started hoisting body bags in litters into the helicopter. The remains were taken to the Rimrock airport for transport by ground vehicles to Yakima.

The NTSB investigation team arrived shortly after and did their investigation with the assistance of the TMRU folks moving aircraft parts. In the process, the final bodies were uncovered and removed to the King County helicopter pickup point.

Preparing a litter to take a body bag to the helicopter. Connie Buchanan in the plaid shirt and white helmet, Fran Sharp (TMRU) in the red helmet.

Hoisting a loaded litter to the Huey. The King County crew chief is wearing the flight suit and standing beyond the litter. Steve Allen (Seattle MR) is holding the tag line to prevent the litter from spinning while being hoisted up to the helicopter. Jeff Sharp (Tacoma Mountain Rescue) in the left yellow parka, SMR wearing the red ones.

CHAPTER 4

CWMR

DURING MY FIFTY-EIGHT years in the field for Mountain Rescue, I have been deputized by a total of five Yakima County Sheriffs and two Coroners based upon my training and my policy of being ready for almost any mission. I have responded to almost all kinds of missions. I have participated in Mountain Rescue training more often as a trainer than as a student, with much of my training having occurred in other venues.

This is a recounting of a few more of the well over 300 missions I have responded to in those fifty-eight years. Some were simple carry-outs or were turned around when the missing person walked out, but all the ones counted required at least some preparation time and/or mileage traveled. Missions varied from routine to the tension of two different helicopter missions into the mountains where the helicopters were actually damaged in flight. On one mission to Mt. Rainier, the extreme turbulence damaged the helicopter so severely in flight (a wrinkle in the tail boom) that after dropping the team on Mt. Ruth (a peak on the ridge of Steamboat Prow) and returning to base, it had to be hauled back to Ft. Lewis on a truck (page79). On another mission, the pilot was trying to land the CWMR team onto a ridge between two trees. During the insertion, the rotor blade tips hit one of the trees and started the separation (delamination) of the blades at their tips. The team was dropped off lower down on the mountain at their request. When the helicopter returned to the base LZ, it was red tagged because of the damage and was hauled back to Ft. Lewis on a truck. On the first mission, the Army flew another helicopter to the scene to pick up the team at the end of the day; the other mission resulted in a walkout, carrying the patient in a litter.

An early mission of CWMR was to investigate an aircraft that had crashed on the north side of Mt. Adams. A hiking party was crossing the glaciers at the base of the mountain when they spotted the tattered remains of an old Piper J-3 Cub, partly melted out from the winter snows. This was another of those summers where the sun was melting snow that had been accumulating for many winters. It was reported that the bones of the pilot were still in the airplane. CWMR sent a team in to recover the remains. The vertical stabilizer of the aircraft was recovered from the wreck, so the team found the aircraft "N" number (the identification number of each airplane). After gathering up the scattered bones from around the pilot's seat, we found that we had all the major bones and most of the minor bones of the body except for the skull and one femur. The bones were carried out from the mountain in a plastic bag. Upon return to Yakima, the Sheriff's Office called Washington State Aeronautics to discuss the find. When Washington State Aeronautics had the "N" number, they were able to look it up and told the Sheriff's deputy in charge of that mission that the plane had crashed in about 1946 and had been found a couple of years later. No one had marked the plane (as they started doing a few years later), but it was reported that the body of the pilot (who had been flying to his wedding) had been brought out and his funeral had been held in his hometown. The north side of Mt. Adams was a long way from the nearest road back in the 1940s, and it was suspected that carrying the head of the pilot out was enough for the folks who had found the wreck.

❖ ❖ ❖

On 15 April 1966, as a member of CWMR, I was invited to a meeting of the Yakima Eagles organization for a presentation. They had read of many of the missions that CWMR had accomplished and presented a plaque to CWMR for CWMR's contributions to the citizens of Central Washington. A photo of the plaque follows.

The Eagles plaque.

The rescue of Russell Post of MRC occurred in July of 1968 on a climb he was making with some Seattle climbers on the west ridge of Mt. Stuart. Russ broke through a snow bridge while climbing just below the summit and fractured his leg. CWMR members from Yakima and Ellensburg participated in the rescue by climbing north over Longs Pass, down into the Ingalls Creek valley, and up Mt. Stuart before the helicopter could get into the scene. As can be seen in the photo, the ceiling (bottom of the clouds) was rather low to the south that day. This was one of the few times Mountain Rescue got to work with an Air Force Kaman "Husky" helicopter. When the ceiling got high enough, the helicopter had to cross Snoqualmie Pass at a low level, fly over Blewett Pass, then it could finally fly up the Ingalls Creek drainage to get to the scene of the accident and lift Russ out from the side of Mt. Stuart.

Loading Russ Post into the Kaman "Husky" helicopter just below the summit of Mt. Stuart. Notice the low cloud bases to the south of the mountain in the background.

❖ ❖ ❖

Well after the hunting season was over in Yakima County, on 23 December 1968, the weather was very cold with two feet or more of snow on the ground. A fellow, apparently hunting, got hypothermic, took off his boots, and continued walking until he collapsed under a tree. Several CWMR teams went into the forest looking for him. The team I was on found him just before dark late in the afternoon and radioed in his location. Another team brought in packs with a litter, tent, and warming equipment. The hunter's feet were both frozen hard. Tapping them with a knife handle was like tapping a rock. His body temperature was so low that we had to bring his temperature up several degrees before we could safely move him.

Presentation by Governor Dan Evans in his office to CWMR members from Yakima and Ellensburg for saving the life of a hunter in the mountains near Yakima. Left to right: Jim Carlson, Judy Beehler, Lee Henkle, Dan Graff, Lynn Buchanan, Jack Powell, Dale Newman, Governor Evans, Curt Julstrud. Washington State photo.

Thurs July 31, 1969

Governor Presents Lifesaving Award

On July 10, Gov. Dan Evans presented the first Governor's Civil Defense Search and Rescue Lifesaving Award. The award was accepted by Lynn Buchanan for the Central Washington Unit, Mountain Rescue Council for their rescue of a young Yakima man lost near Chinook Pass. Buchanan is the son of Mr. and Mrs. L. L. Buchanan of Selah.

Separated from companions while cougar hunting on Dec. 21, 1968, 25-year-old Lonnie Killian of Yakima became lost near the Naches Ranger Station on Chinook Pass.

The incident was reported to Kittitas County Sheriff Bob Barret. Under the direction of Sheriff Barret, a search of the area began on Dec. 22. With temperatures in the low 20's and 30-inches of snow on the ground, the search continued for 38 hours before Killian was located. He was found sitting under a tree on the nearly bare ground, evidence that he had been there for some time. He was barefoot, had discarded several items of clothing and was suffering from extreme exposure. His eyes were dilated and he mumbled incoherently. His temperature was 82 degrees.

Immediate life-saving measures were applied and after five hours his temperature was raised to 94 degrees, at which time he was evacuated to the nearest road and immediately moved to a Yakima hospital. Members of an Explorer Scout Search and Rescue Unit from the Ellensburg area assisted in the search and evacuation.

Thorough investigation of the incident by Hal Foss, state civil defense search and rescue coordinator, clearly determined that the victim would have died within a short period of time if the members of the Central Washington Unit, Mountain Rescue Council had not prepared themselves by knowledge, training and proper equipment in the techniques of arresting the effects of hypothermia (exposure) in the field.

The Central Washington Unit, Mountain Rescue Council, is based in Eastern Washington with the bulk of its membership in the Yakima area, but with others in the Ellensburg and Wenatchee vicinity. It has about 50 members on its active roster, with approximately 30 of them fully qualified and experienced mountain rescue members.

ADDING MACHINE TAPE, stamp pads, envelopes, stationery. SELAH VALLEY OPTIMIST.

Article from Selah Valley Optimist.

We put him into a sleeping bag in the tent and warmed him in the field with a portable space heater that CWMR had carried in with the litter. Dr. Jim Dodge and I were in charge of warming his body while keeping his feet frozen so they could be warmed in the hospital. After his core temperature was up to almost normal and he could be moved, we called an ambulance to the road end and transported him several miles in a Stokes litter to the ambulance. Everyone went back to Yakima, mission accomplished.

When the fellow revived in the hospital, however, he complained that one of the rescuers had stolen his wallet. The deputy came down to where we were cleaning and repacking our equipment and told us the story with appropriate comments. We dumped the sleeping bag we had carried him in and there was his wallet—it contained only his welfare papers! He recovered from his ordeal with only the loss of several of his toes.

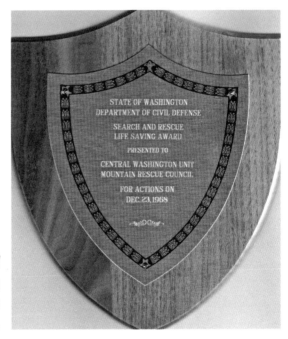

Plaque awarded to CWMR for saving the life on the above mission.

❖ ❖ ❖

On 1 July 1972, a twin-engine Cessna, contracted to the US Forest Service to carry smokejumpers from Troutdale Airport in Oregon to the airport at Winthrop, crashed on the east side of the north ridge of Mt. Adams on its return trip. The pilot was killed. CWMR sent several members to pick up the body and escort one of the FAA investigators to the scene. The mission involved two days and two trips in a Huey. On the first trip, late in the afternoon, it became particularly interesting when the Huey fuel pump quit as the helicopter was offloading us onto a pinnacle on the north ridge at 10,400 feet. We jumped out of the door of the bird and lay on the flat top of the rock while the pilot slid the Huey forward with just enough power to clear the rock. He then dropped down the mountain to pick up enough airspeed for level flight without overtaxing the fuel system. He returned to Yakima and arranged for another Huey to pick us up later.

We found a route to the crash site, then located the body of the pilot and put it in a body bag. The pilot had been thrown through the windscreen and was located about fifty feet up the rocky slope beyond the aircraft. We had to be back on the ridge before dark to be picked up by the helicopter, so after a preliminary look around the area, we climbed back up to the LZ.

We radioed the Yakima Sheriff's Office (YSO) to be picked up by a helicopter. A brisk wind blew on the mountain all afternoon, but the wind began bringing moisture in and caused a lenticular cloud to form on the top of Mt. Adams as we were climbing back to the top of the ridge. While we were climbing, the cloud descended below the pickup altitude. As a result, we had to descend to clear air. We called the YSO to hold the helicopter until we could find another landing zone. The FAA fellow commented that it was not really cold. "Why not just stay there on the mountain until morning?" he asked. We, with more weather experience at altitude, were more interested in getting off the mountain. When we got below the cloud, the best LZ we could see in the dark was the lower part of Adams Glacier at about 8,000 feet, so we called for the Huey and worked our way down onto the glacier. The surface of the glacier at that point was close to level, so the team marked out a location with our headlamps. The Huey arrived with all its lights on and hovered above the surface of the glacier as we all moved over to climb in. It was pretty spectacular in the dark with small ice crystals being thrown into the air in the downwash of the rotors and being illuminated by the red-and-green navigation lights of the Huey as well as by the white landing lights.

We returned to Yakima and arranged an early morning pickup to return to the scene on Mt. Adams. Back on the mountain the next morning, the helicopter used the same 10, 400-foot LZ.

I pointed out to the FAA fellow the eighth of an inch of ice on the windward side of all the rocks. He admitted that it would have been rather uncomfortable huddling there all night without tents and sleeping bags. Then we belayed the FAA fellow down the ten-foot cliff and back over to the remains of the aircraft, which was resting on a steep scree slope. Some of the smaller pieces of the wreckage had fallen to the lower part of Lava Glacier and were unreachable, but he was interested in looking at the instruments. I located the pilot's yoke, which had the autopilot switch turned on. It was later found that the pilot had been flying for about eighteen hours that day and the decision was that he had fallen asleep with the autopilot on. With the strong west wind, the plane had drifted too far east for the autopilot to correct the course and the plane had impacted the north side of Mt. Adams slightly above 10,000 feet.

We carried the remains of the pilot to the top of the rock at the 10,400-foot LZ. The Mountain Rescue folks all had their climbing food with them for lunch. The FAA fellow had not brought anything. Since he had no food, everyone offered him a bit of their supply. Back in Yakima, I later heard him describing his lunch to his partner. He was exclaiming over the things he had eaten there on the mountain: smoked clams and oysters, smoked octopus tentacle, sardines, crackers, cheese, peanut butter and jelly sandwich, "It was like being in a delicatessen!"

The Huey came back, picked up the Mountain Rescue Team, the FAA fellow, and the body bag, and then returned everyone to McAllister's Fixed Base Operation (FBO) at the Yakima airport. Another mission successfully completed with two hours flight time in the UH-1H.

On 7 February 1973, Wednesday, Central Washington Mountain Rescue was alerted for a search of the east side of Mt. Adams for two climbers whose announced goal was to climb the Wilson Icefall in the winter. This mission turned into one of the longest and most involved missions accomplished by Central. On the first day of the search, eight to ten CWMR searchers went in by vehicle to the southeast corner of Mt. Adams, then were taken up on the east side of the mountain by folks from the Ski-Benders Snowmobile Club. The Ski-Benders took us as high as they could on the first day, then we continued on foot, climbing high on Wilson Glacier.

The search continued through a second day before everyone was evacuated from the mountain and returned home after spending forty-eight hours on the mission. We had found no evidence indicating the two climbers we were looking for were on the mountain.

A lot of discussion about where the climbers could be ensued, but nothing further was found. On 16 February 1973, arrangements were made for several other CWMR members and myself to ride to the base of the mountain on Thiokol snow machines from the Yakama Indian Nation. The Nation had two

Air Force surplus machines and thought they could get two teams of us to the mountain farther to the north than the area that had already been searched. A long day was spent in the field on the Thiokol machines, but they couldn't get very close to the mountain, primarily because there was a lot of forested area between the end of the roads and the base of the mountain.

Mt. Adams, north side, in the winter. North Ridge is the prominent ridge descending directly toward the viewer of the picture. High Camp is just beyond the rocky ridge in the very lower right corner of the picture. Lava Glacier is to the left of North Ridge in this view, and Lyman Glacier is left of the Lava. Wilson Glacier is just this side of the left skyline ridge. Adams Glacier and Icefall is to the right of North Ridge, and Northwest Ridge is to the right of that, to the middle of the right side of the photo. Aerial photo by LKB.

*The northeast side of Mt. Adams through the windshield of a
Huey helicopter (UH-1) en route to the search area
at the base of Wilson and Lyman Glaciers.*

Four days later, Tuesday, 20 February, in an air search of the
mountain, what appeared to be a body was spotted at about
10,000 feet lying on a pinnacle of ice among some seracs on the
upper Lyman Glacier.

Six of us members of CWMR were flown in by an Army Huey
and dropped off at about 8,200 feet on a relatively flat area below
the glacier. We climbed to the reported spot; indeed the body of
one of the climbers was lying there. It was apparent that the two
climbers had fallen from higher on Lyman. One had impacted
on the ice pinnacle and died there. The climber's rope extended
down the ice past the pinnacle and was untied at the end; one of
them had survived the fall and left the accident scene.

Clint Crocker and Judy Beehler climbing up Lyman Glacier to reach the serac where one of the bodies had been spotted from the helicopter.

Additional climbers from CWMR were ferried by snowmobiles to the landing zone just west of the long moraine at the toe of the Lyman, then they climbed part way to the scene, leaving the machines and drivers to await their return. We lowered the body approximately 1,000 feet down to the second team, then both teams finished lowering the frozen body another 1,000 feet or so to the snow machine pickup point, arriving there just as it got dark. The body was fastened on a sled so it could be towed out to the road by one of the snowmobiles.

The mountain rescue team at the scene where the first climber's body was found. His body is in front of the two MR folks at the left. His climbing rope extends beyond the serac down and to the lower left corner of the photo. Note the snow being blown over the ridge in the background by the strong winds that afternoon.

Starting to lower the body off the top of the serac and down the glacier. There is a snowmobile down by the moraine in the distance, just a black speck on the distant snowfield. The second body was found in the snow-covered rocky area seen at the top of this photo.

In the photograph above, one of the snowmobiles can be seen as a tiny speck just to the left of the serac that has the body. The snowmobile is almost 2,000 feet below where the folks are standing. There are two or three more Mountain Rescue folks standing on the ridge below the serac and to the right of the rock pinnacle. The other snow machines are out of sight behind the serac or the ridge just below us. The ridge beyond the snowmobile is the moraine below Lyman Glacier.

The Ski-Benders brought enough snowmobiles to take all the Mountain Rescue folks back to the road. The snow machine trip, in the dark of the night, back to the cars was not without event. A couple of times a machine went over a small ridge and found a hole on the other side, which trapped the machine until several folks could get together and pull it out. On a steep irregular slope, the sled with the body tied on it passed the snow machine that was pulling it. As the sled slid downhill past the slower snow machine, the victim's foot booted the passenger, Mountain Rescue member Judy Beehler, off the snow machine she was riding!

After a bit of scrambling to get the machines stopped to reload on the steep slope, everyone got back on to continue the trip out. The snow machine route extended to the southeast corner of the mountain in the Yakama Indian Reservation. The vehicles on the road were reached in the very early morning. As with most late-night rescue completions, because rescues are not planned ahead of time, the incentive to get home to go to work in the morning resulted in another long late drive home, arriving there in the wee hours of the morning as daylight was showing over the hills to the east.

The second body was found the next day some distance below that moraine when it was spotted by a helicopter searching the shortest distance down the mountain from the accident site.

Lowering the body down Lyman Glacier. The person in the blue helmet is lowering the body while the person in the Mountain Rescue parka is belaying him. There are two of the backup team visible on the ridge beyond. The snowmobiles are behind and another 1,000 feet below them.

The autopsy of the second victim revealed he had a severely broken leg and had probably crawled to reach the point where he was found, a couple of miles from where he had untied from the rope.

A camera was found with one of the victims. When the film was developed, it had pictures of their camp located somewhere in the trees. The camp was not found, nor were their skis found. Pictures they had taken during the climb showed their climbing route had been on Wilson Glacier.

This multiday search was the longest in the records of CWMR to that time. It involved snowmobiles, Thiokol snow machines, helicopters, and climbers on several possible routes on Mt. Adams. Agencies involved included Yakima County Sheriff's Office,

Yakama Indian Agency, the US Army Aviation Branch, Central Washington Mountain Rescue, Ski-Benders Snowmobile Club, as well as some private pilots and the use of personal vehicles for transportation.

On 23 February, the body of the second victim was found lower on the mountain, below the terminal moraine of Lyman and Wilson Glaciers. The body was recovered by an Army helicopter with two Sheriff's Deputies, Maurice Rice, and Lynn Buchanan on board.

My Mountain Rescue hours on this mission were:
7 February: 24 hours – Search.
8 February: 24 hours – Search
16 February: 12 hours – Search
21 February: 24 hours – Body Recovery
23 February: 1 hour – Body Recovery
Total: Eighty-five hours for one individual (myself). At least ten persons were on the mission on each of the first four days, working a similar amount of hours, plus the snowmobile drivers, YSO personnel, and others involved. During that time, all the miles traveled on the highway were in personal vehicles.

The shoulder patch of the Ski-Benders Snowmobile Club.
A great group on several Mt. Adams missions.
The patch is from Pinky Paxton.

Getting the machines ready to move in
to recover the first body on Mt. Adams.

Break time en route.

❖ ❖ ❖

In August of 1975, two aircraft accidents occurred in the Cascade Mountains on the same Sunday evening. CWMR was dispatched to one, MRC to the other. We from CWMR were taken by helicopter to the top of the ridge a hundred feet above the aircraft in the photo below. It was located just north of Chinook Pass and west of Gold Hill. We were left there, and the helicopter went to Seattle to pick up some Seattle MRC members to locate the other crash near Snoqualmie Pass.

In the accident assigned to CWMR, the two pilots in the plane were flying VFR (visual flying rules) from the west under an overcast sky. They had only a few feet to climb to get over the ridge, but when they climbed, they got into the clouds. They then lost visual contact with the ground, lost control of the aircraft, and came out of the clouds in a spin. They impacted the ground at ninety degrees to the surface. The plane collapsed to approximately seven feet long from the front of the engine to the highest point of the tail. The original length was just over thirty feet. A hunter observed the impact, hiked out, and called the YSO, who then dispatched CWMR. The NTSB (National Transportation and Safety Board) was advised and an agent of theirs went with CWMR on the helicopter trip to the scene. That agency's interest was probably because both the victims in the airplane were FAA employees from the Boise airport tower. The CWMR members were helping remove the metal of the aircraft so they could get inside to the bodies. As I removed one piece of metal, my hand grasped a reddish orange piece of flesh. This caused a bit of consternation until someone remarked that the victims had been salmon fishing. The salmon flesh from the cargo space behind the seats was mixed with the bodies.

CWMR members and an NTSB agent examining the crash of a Cessna 182 north of Chinook Pass that took the lives of two FAA tower employees returning to Boise from fishing on the coast. The plane impacted at ninety degrees to the ground surface.

While the bodies were being removed and placed in body bags, the NTSB agent examined the wreckage. He then called in on his radio and everyone was picked up by a helicopter and transported to the Crystal Mountain Ski Area Parking lot. From there the seven CWMR members were picked up by two vehicles from Yakima and returned home. This was another of several aircraft accidents I have observed where the airplane was flying very close to the ridge top, but just below the cloud level. The pilot needed another fifty feet to clear it safely. When he climbed the extra distance, he was in the clouds and lost visual orientation, followed by losing control of the airplane.

As a side note, a similar accident occurred in Okinawa in 1955 when a USAF B-50 was making low-level airdrops for practice at night on the beach east of Kadena AFB. After the drop, the aircraft went over a plateau south of the beach. When the pilot realized he was over the plateau and far too low, he pulled back sharply on the wheel to climb. The tail of the aircraft made an imprint in the soft dirt of a cultivated field, then the tail snapped off. The aircraft tumbled end over end and was destroyed, as was the crew. I was sent to the scene at daybreak with a photographer to record the accident.

On 7 March 1976, I received an interesting call from the Yakima County Sheriff's Office with a mission, if I could handle it. They had gotten a phone call from the Yakima Health District telling them that they had a report from a doctor that there was an extremely sick family at the hospital.

It seems that the family had been out at the county landfill and found a large pile of wheat there. It looked like clean wheat, so they had taken a lot of it home and ground most of it up for food. They had also fed some to their chickens. Now, after eating the flour and the eggs, they were all very sick. Someone from the Health District went to the landfill and found what was left of the wheat, brought it in, and tested it. It had residue of a mercury compound on it. When they found that out, they checked and found that a wheat rancher had dumped a large quantity of seed wheat at the landfill. The seed had been treated with a mercury compound to kill the pests that might eat it, but the farmer did not plant it for some reason.

The health district staff had taken tissue, blood, and hair samples from the family members and wanted to get the samples and a wheat sample to Rochester, New York, as fast as possible for testing. They were arranging for a F-102 fighter aircraft to fly the samples from Geiger Air Force Base (now Geiger Field, Spokane International Airport), and it would be ready to go in another couple of hours. The problem was how to get the samples to Geiger by the time the fighter plane was ready to go.

I told YSO that if they would take the samples to the airport, I could be ready in a few minutes to fly them to Spokane in my Cherokee 6. It would take just over an hour's flying time for me. I called Judy Beehler and asked if she would meet me at the airport and copilot the trip with me. She readily agreed. I met a sheriff's deputy at the airport who gave me the small cardboard box of samples, and we took off. The weather was great and just over an hour later, we were landing at Geiger Field. The tower directed us to the National Guard side of the airport where an F-102 was being readied for the flight. (We had a great opportunity to look over the F-102 [Voodoo] as the ground crew was completing its preparation for the flight.) The squadron insignia was an ace of spades playing card with a dagger through it. We handed over the box of samples, then made the trip back to Yakima. Another mission (although somewhat different) was accomplished.

❖ ❖ ❖

On 17 Jul 1976, a climber had fallen high on Mt. Adams and was last seen by his partner as he went out of sight, sliding down the steep snow slope of the upper Northwest Ridge. The partner descended the mountain without seeing him, hiked three miles from High Camp on the north side of Mt. Adams to the road, and then drove to Packwood or Randle where he called the Yakima County Sheriff's Office just before daylight. A MAST Huey helicopter was dispatched early in the morning with two Central Washington Mountain Rescue (CWMR) members on board, Judy Beehler and me. After almost two hours of aerial searching, the subject was spotted at a rock on the slope. He was wearing a yellow helmet, but the rest of his apparel and his pack were all either brown or black, very close to the color of the rocks. The helicopter hovered over a nearby rock pinnacle to offload the Mountain Rescue folks, who then roped up and chopped steps across the steep snow slope to the chap who was lying on his stomach, clinging to a rock. He had tumbled down the snow slope well over a thousand feet, losing his ice axe in the process. He was still conscious after almost twenty hours of lying there but was not inclined to let go of the rock. Since we were unable to take the rock with us, we tied him to our rope, assured him of his security, and belayed him back across the slope to the pinnacle. While we were doing this, the helicopter went back to Yakima to refuel, then returned to hover close and pick up all three of us, introducing the fall victim to an even less secure feeling.

When the fall victim, who was not seriously hurt, was asked why he was not wearing brighter clothing, he replied, "That creates visual pollution! He was asked if he objected to the two hours of noise pollution and exhaust gas from the turbine engine of the helicopter that the mountain was subjected to because of his dislike of bright colors. He realized then that the bright yellow color of the helmet had been rather helpful to him. (Some "pollutions" are better than others.)

Klootchman Rock, west side, taken in October 2007. The accident was on the east side of the north end (left end in this picture) on the other side of one of the two lower peaks visible here.

In the late afternoon of 17 October 1977, there was a call for a rescue on a ridge of rock near Yakima. Klootchman Rock is a volcanic dike, rotten and loose but harder than the stuff around it so it stayed when the rest of the area weathered down over the centuries. The climber was dangling from the end of his rope, fifty feet above the base of the cliff. One piton had held, saving him from falling the rest of the way.

CWMR was called for the rescue. Beehler and I were called by the sheriff's office to meet the MAST helicopter at the St. Elizabeth's hospital helicopter pad, pick up some medications and IV solutions, and be ready to climb. We were given the IV fluids and IV administration equipment there and the ER doctor sent some medication (with syringes) along that had to be mixed with sterile saline before being injected. When we arrived at Klootchman Rock and spotted the injured climber, the helicopter hovered above the boulder field at the base of the cliff while the two CWMR folks jumped a few feet to the rocks. My thought was that if one of us broke an ankle on the jump, we at least had immediate evacuation to the hospital available, but then the medic or crew chief would have to make the same jump to get the injured person back into the helicopter. We made it safely. The helicopter flew back to the Yakima airport to pick up a couple more CWMR members and more equipment, then returned to drop them off on the boulder field. After that, the helicopter descended to a clearing in the valley below to wait while another backup team came forty miles from Yakima in the rescue truck.

While the helicopter was in transit, we, the first team, had to climb the cliff to the patient. Judy tried climbing one route; I tried another. We had each tried a couple of routes on the loose rock of Klootchman before Judy found one that would go. Judy led the route while I followed. Both of us free climbed the fifty feet. It was late in the day by the time we reached the patient.

When we got to the injured fellow, we tied him off to the rock to secure him, then did an assessment. During the examination he would recover consciousness periodically for a moment or two and would thrash around frantically. In the process he hit Judy once, almost knocking her off the rock. I called the Yakima County Sheriff's Office with my handheld radio and Sheriff's Dispatch telephoned the hospital to relay the message. I told the doctor that the patient was too combative to keep an IV in, so the doctor suggested the medication first, then an IV when he was off the rock. Judy was below the patient, so she cut a neat round hole in the rear of his climbing pants. I mixed the meds, drew them up into a syringe, then handed the syringe to her. She swabbed his buttock through the hole, injected the medication, then dropped the syringe to the bottom of the cliff for someone to pick up and store safely.

By then the second CWMR team was at the bottom of the rock and a couple of them climbed up to the side of us where they could fix some anchors. "Fix" and "anchor" are relative terms in the rotten lava we had to deal with, but they found something relatively solid where they could affix a pulley. We secured the fellow into a Stokes litter, tensioned the rope to the litter, cut his climbing rope, and then the team members at the base of the cliff lowered him down in the dark as we scrambled off the cliff. When he was at the base of the cliff, we carried him to the helicopter in the valley below. In pitch dark the helicopter lifted off. Since the two of us had ridden up, protocol required that we ride back (so we and the pilot told the rest of the team). The real reason was: WE GOT TO RIDE!

Between a cliff on one side (Goose Egg Mountain), heavy timber, and Klootchman Rock on the other, with only a small patch of stars visible above him, the pilot had to really scramble for air and space above. There were a few moments of serious tension! We made it.

The patient survived the fall with a collapsed lung, head injuries, and several broken ribs. (See *Accidents in North American Mountaineering*,1978, page 36. Published by the American Alpine Club).

The next day I went back to the scene with a couple of hot, young climbers who just scrambled up the rocks to get all the ropes and anchors down. I tried a couple of the routes in the daylight, then had a great idea: "You guys just drop the equipment down, and I will coil and bag it to carry out." That sure beat saying, "I'm too chicken to climb this pile of rotten rock again when I'm not under pressure."

❖ ❖ ❖

I was talking to the counselor at Wapato High School on another of my volunteer duties (as a Liaison Officer for the Air Force Academy) on Thursday morning, 23 March 1978, when I got an emergency call from the Yakima County Sheriff's Office. A climber had fallen five hundred feet down steep snow and ice in the Goat Rocks Wilderness area. He had a fractured hip and punctured chest. At the time of the injury (0900, 22 March 1978), the weather was sunny with a strong wind, but it had now deteriorated to overcast. Lewis County was unable to get a MAST helicopter into the area, so they had called Seattle and Tacoma Mountain Rescue teams in addition to Central (CWMR).

Seattle MRC, with George Sainsbury as Base Operations Leader (OL), established a base of operations in the town of Packwood and had gotten the assistance of the Army to fly team members into the area to lift the patient out. The weather had gotten really bad, with solid clouds and constant snowfall in the higher elevations of the Goat Rocks, making snow travel quite risky due to the possibility of avalanche. The injured climber's two companions had already spent at least a day coming out, so Mountain Rescue was already into the third day since the injury. They reported that the injured climber, Gregg Bennett, was supposedly warm and sort of comfortable in a tent at the scene of the accident.

Several of us CWMR members left the Yakima County Sheriff's Office at 1315 hours on 23 March and drove the seventy miles or so to Packwood to assist the Lewis County Sheriff's Office. CWMR joined the Tacoma and Seattle Mountain Rescue Teams in Packwood. George assigned teams from the members of the three Mountain Rescue organizations based on their skills. Some were to fly in with the helicopters, and two teams were scheduled to go to the west side of the Goat Rocks the next morning to try to get to the scene of the accident on foot.

As the teams were gathering in Packwood, the two helicopters assigned to the mission by Ft. Lewis arrived at Packwood airport. At the time, I had been volunteering to fly with the 54th Medical Detachment (MAST) at Ft. Lewis three or four weekends each summer, so I was known to several of the pilots of the Third of the Fifth (3/5th), the unit that brought in the helicopters. I had a helicopter helmet belonging to my younger brother, Douglas, and was able to converse with the crew, so I was assigned to ride in the first helicopter to go flying that afternoon. A team of Dave Rowland, Craig Eilers, and Tom Hickman loaded into the helicopter with me. The pilot flew us in over a road west of Packwood with the idea of finding a valley extending toward the patient's location. He flew close to the right-hand side of the canyon wall at just over the treetops to stay under the clouds (what the Army called "Nap of the Earth" flying). The pilot came to a large treeless spot on the ridge—all white—just as a sudden flurry of snow covered the windshield. The pilot lost visual reference (called "Inadvertent Instrument Meteorological Conditions," or "IMC"), turned away from the canyon wall, went into the clouds, stalled the aircraft, then fell out of the clouds almost inverted and pointing down canyon (a 180-degree change of direction). It felt like a half hour in the clouds but was probably not more than five to ten seconds. The pilot got the Huey right side up and flying again just before the skids got to the treetops! As a fixed-wing pilot, I really thought we had bought the proverbial farm.

Since I was wearing the helicopter helmet, I heard the pilots admit to each other that they thought the same! The pilots returned to Packwood since that canyon climbed right up into the clouds prohibiting access from that direction. (The question was asked, "Did they need to change their shorts, also?")

The pilots decided to send another crew and helicopter farther west and see what the clouds were like up that valley. After a team including myself loaded on that bird, it took off and flew more southwesterly from Packwood. Since it was farther west, maybe it could get around the clouds bunched against the high ridge of the Goat Rocks. The theory was good. At one point, the pilot could see blue sky through a small hole in the clouds, so he climbed at maximum rate through the hole. It closed as he was climbing and we were in IMC for the second time that afternoon. In this case, the pilot knew where he was in relation to the mountains, so he could climb on instruments, heading west, which would get him away from all of the high terrain. He called Seattle Center (radar) for a clearance from his present position to Sea-Tac. He got an instrument clearance and climbed to 12,000 feet through the clouds heading west. That altitude put us above the clouds.

Photo showing the back of Doug's helmet. It served a tour in Viet Nam with Doug and many missions on MAST helicopters with Lynn. The snakeskin glued on the left is from a tiny poisonous Viet Nam snake. Doug's crew chief from those days recognized it at Ft. Lewis one day. He said he flew many missions in 'Nam behind that helmet.

From on top of the clouds, the pilot got a look at the ridge near the patient's tent but was unable to fly to it because the fast-moving clouds kept obscuring the peaks. There was a plume of snow blowing about a quarter mile straight out from one of the peaks in the area and the turbulence over the clouds was pretty bad (severe turbulence). The pilot spent quite a while on top looking for another hole to get back down—he even talked about an instrument approach to Gray Field at Ft. Lewis if he couldn't find a hole. At decision time, another hole opened up in the clouds ("sucker hole" in pilot's parlance), so he cancelled his instrument clearance and took the Huey down—at over 3,000 feet per minute. He and the copilot were talking about keeping the rotor blades from overspeeding as they dropped. An overspeed caution light was lighted during most of the descent toward the highway. The hole in the clouds kept closing and opening during the descent. We came down sort of like a rock falling, but he got below the clouds and we could follow the highway back to Packwood. One of the mountain rescue fellows from the coast didn't know how to Valsalva to clear his ears and ended up with an ear injury from that ride.

That was enough flying for the afternoon. The Lewis County Sheriff's Office arranged rooms for the Mountain Rescue teams in the old Packwood Hotel for the night. The hotel had recently been refurbished to what it was in about 1900. Each small room had wood paneling, a twin bed, dresser, hanger hook on the back of the door, and a toilet at the end of the hall. The accommodations were a lot nicer than a sleeping bag in a tent! The Sheriff bought dinner that night for all the teams, and the wake-up call came before daylight. When the teams got up at 0300 hours, the deputy had arranged with a restaurant to serve breakfast to the twenty to thirty Mountain Rescue folks on scene.

One Huey lifted at daybreak (about 0600) with Clint Crocker (CWMR) and the eyewitness (a member of the party who had hiked out with the news). The pilot found a hole in the clouds and got to within one and one half miles of Elk Pass, where he landed and dropped the two fellows. Then the weather closed in and the pilot stated that he was lucky to get back. The wind on the ridge was about fifty knots with lots of blowing new snow.

Hotel Packwood in January 2011.

Crocker and the injured climber's partner went to the scene from their LZ to care for the injured climber. Another Mountain Rescue team was taken up the road on a Thiokol to make a conventional approach to Beargrass Flats from the west. They were to go to 3,200 feet and hike in on snowshoes with two more four-man teams following them.

When the first Huey returned, both Hueys each loaded four Mountain Rescue members. One team included an Army doctor with mountain climbing experience and equipment. Both birds flew up the Packwood Lake Valley, which ends in a very steep-walled cirque, mostly cliffs. As they flew up the valley, they were in and out of the bottom of the clouds, occasionally losing sight of each other as they tried to find a way over the top of the east wall of the valley. The rotor noise of the two helicopters was knocking big avalanches down and over the cliffs beside us. I counted seven major avalanches running, others saw more. The helicopter I was riding in finally found a shallow pass in the ridge to the east and after more than an hour of flying, the pilot was able to drop us near a rock outcrop. The pilot hovered about a foot off the snow while we jumped out. We had all had been told to never grab a helicopter winch cable until the hook touches the ground, but this was not a cable operation. The Huey was hovering in dry snow conditions with powder snow blowing all around. We all jumped out into the deep snow and the crew chief pushed the (steel) Stokes litter for the patient part way out of the door. As the bird was hovering and stirring up a dense cloud of powder snow, he gestured for one of the team to grab the litter. I was waving for him to drop it, but he apparently felt it would be lost in the snow and wanted someone to have it in hand. I knew that the rotors would be building a huge static charge around the Huey and the blowing snow would make it even worse. With nothing being accomplished and the helicopter just waiting, I reached up to grab the steel Stokes litter containing my ice axe and pack. I found it was like grabbing a live high-voltage wire! I found myself on my back looking up at the helicopter. It took three tries by others to get the equipment out—very painful tries. Someone had to do it; we could have been dead without the equipment in that storm if anything went wrong. When the crew finally realized why we kept falling down, they threw the Stokes litter and the rest of the gear to the ground. Two fellows had left their ice axes in the helicopter and three did not bring crampons, expecting deep new snow. The teams roped up to prevent an accident on the ice-hard, wind-packed slopes of the ridge. I roped up with J. Kassuba and M. Waller of MRC. (Martin Waller and I had been on the MRC Arctic trip earlier in the year.) It took over two hours to travel the two miles to the accident scene near the top of the ridge in the storm. At one point we reversed rope leads after the leader led out onto an exposed avalanche slope. It was a dicey 150-foot retreat to firmer snow.

When we reached the tent, the doctor took charge of the patient. One of the rescuers was rapidly getting hypothermic, so another two rescuers had to take care of him while most of the rest of us were involved in preparing to evacuate the patient to an LZ. I took a rope team to scout an LZ and a safe route to it. Taking the patient back the way we had arrived would have meant that both the rescuers and the patient would be on some long exposed traverses on the icy snow of the canyon in the battering wind and (literally) blinding snow. The accident had occurred near the top center of a huge accumulation zone rapidly filling with unconsolidated snow. The first attempt to find a route took us onto a beautiful convex slope with a foot of wind-packed snow over several feet of damp, loose snow. We retreated without anything sliding. The next try was a traverse to the south ridge above Packwood Lake with ten feet or so of loose snow at thirty to thirty-five degrees. We followed the ridge down vertically for about 700 feet on wind-packed snow. Visibility ahead was about ten feet most of the time, but the ridge at the end of the cirque above Packwood Lake with trees on the edge of it was visible when the clouds would lift occasionally for a few moments. At the bottom of the bowl, I had to lead across an old avalanche gully that looked about ten to twelve feet wide but was hard to see in the blowing snow. After sinking to our waists a couple of times, we put on snowshoes, climbed back up a little, and started down the side of the gully. It seemed to go down forever, and we soon lost perspective as the sides blocked out the view. We became rather concerned to get out of the gully and were amazed to find that it was more than thirty feet deep and a hundred feet wide—rapidly filling with new snow. We marked a route and returned to the tent.

When the patient was stabilized and ready to move, we wrapped him in his sleeping bag and some plastic to keep him warm and dry. We secured him in the Stokes litter and started down the route we had located. When we reached the large gully, there was no other way to go, so we rigged a traveling pulley and when the litter reached the bottom, we hooked on and hauled it out at rather high speed. When it looked like we were going to reach the ridge top with a bit of visibility under the clouds, we radioed Packwood for the helicopters.

Both Hueys arrived very shortly, just under the bottom of the clouds, so one was waved in to the LZ on the ridge. He held a hover while the Mountain Rescue folks loaded the patient, his gear, and five people in. (Each rescuer had a forty- to fifty-pound pack also.) With three crewmen and at 6,000 feet of altitude, that was a bit of an overload! When that helicopter left, the second one moved in. It was getting dark, so I planned to have the last two of us rescuers hike out, but the pilot flagged all seven on board. The pilot lifted off, then edged the Huey out over the cliff and dropped almost to the valley bottom as he exchanged altitude for flying speed. He was just over the treetops around Packwood Lake when he leveled out and flew to the Packwood airport.

At Packwood, the teams sorted gear, had another dinner on the Lewis County Sheriff, and then drove home. Some of us CWMR folks arrived in Yakima at 2200 hours Friday night. Others of the team stayed another night in Packwood to await the foot teams who were camping at 6,200 feet until Saturday morning. When they reached Packwood that afternoon, then returned home, the mission was successfully closed.

My mission data:

Helicopter flight time: 4.5 hours
POV travel miles: 144
Personal hours: 37.0
Hiking miles: Not tracked, mostly in heavy fog and blowing snow.

❖ ❖ ❖

One of the early helicopter missions CWMR participated in was for a hiker who was injured in the high country west of Goose Prairie. A team from CWMR was flown into the area in a Huey to help locate and bring out an injured person. This was sometime after Beehler and I had started flying regularly on the MAST standby weekends. I was not on this mission but heard about it from one of the helicopter crewmembers later. As the helicopter was returning to Yakima, the OL (CWMR Operations Leader for the mission) was in the helicopter facing aft. He was making another count of personnel, making sure that the whole team was aboard. He could not see Judy, but all the rest of the team was visible. The Crew Chief saw him looking around rather frantically and asked him what was wrong. The OL said one of the team was missing-—the lady they had with them. The MAST Crew Chief laughed and said, "Do you mean Judy?" "Yes!" "She is flying the helicopter!" Sure enough, there she was, riding in a pilot's seat! It was quite a shock to the male ego. The OL was one of those who didn't want to go on the Ft. Lewis MAST standby teams—helicopters were just too dangerous!

On 19 Oct 1987, CWMR was dispatched to search for a blind elk hunter somewhere west of the Ahtanum ranger station. It sounded a bit strange, but when the teams got to the end of the road, near the crest of the Cascades, it was determined that even though the hunter was classified as legally blind, he really had some peripheral vision and was able to hunt, even though he had to work at seeing. He had hunted west of the car while his hunting companions had gone other directions. When he did not return that night, his companions had waited until morning to call the Yakima County Sheriff's Office and get a search started for him.

Quite a few CWMR members were in the field and started walking down the mountains to the west from the car. Early in the afternoon, an Army Chinook helicopter arrived and picked up three CWMR members, including myself, to search farther west than the foot troops could. Someone had reported seeing some smoke across the valley. The valley bottom had a small river, a rapidly moving stream, and no one thought the hunter would have crossed that and gone up the steep hillside beyond, but the helicopter was requested to check out the smoke. Once over the smoke, we saw a fire in the middle of a forest road with a fellow waving frantically at the helicopter. A Chinook requires a bigger LZ than does a Huey, but one was located a quarter mile or so to the west of the fire, and the CWMR team ran through the brush and trees to the location of the fire.

The fellow was trying to get the fire out when we got there and was very happy to greet the CWMR team. This was indeed the hunter for whom we had been searching. He had gone farther than he had intended and could not determine which way he had to go to get back to the car. He thought he was going toward the car, but when he crossed the river, he knew he had made a mistake. He decided to go uphill. However, he went farther west instead of going east. As it was getting dark, he found a road and while walking on it, spotted a book of paper matches lying on it. He knew he was lost, so he stopped walking and built a fire to keep warm for the night.

When the sun came up, he added fir boughs to the fire to make it big and to make a lot of smoke. We helped him put the fire out, loaded him into the Chinook, and took him back to his friends and their car. He said that he had seen a large bull elk, but he knew he was lost at that time so had to let it go on its way.

This was a strange mission, but one that ended happily and gave me another 1.4 hours of helicopter flight. This time it was in a Chinook helicopter with the call sign "Freight Train."

❖ ❖ ❖

On 11 August 1996, CWMR was called out to search for a hiker who had not returned from a hike on the north side of Mt. Adams. It became an all-out search involving the SAR folks as well as CWMR. Todd Braman was searching from the air in his C-172, and later the King County Sheriff's Office sent their UH-1B helicopter and a few of their folks trained in aerial searching to the scene.

By this time in the history of CWMR, the State of Washington had developed a certification program to train those who would need to ride in helicopters, teaching safety and skills necessary for the personnel who would be riding and working around them. I had been trained by the US Army 54th Medical Detachment at Ft. Lewis and had been a trainer for the MAST program. I had some fifty helicopter missions by then and 6,000 hours of fixed-wing flying, but I was not considered properly trained by the state program officials. Since I had not received the official "State Helicopter Training," I was being used as a ground-pounder by CWMR, hiking up to High Camp (the climbers' camping area) at tree line on Mt. Adams and searching down the mountain. At one point I was directed to a snowfield at a particular location to look at some tracks spotted from below by some SAR folks with binoculars. After considerable discussion on the radio, we determined the location given was well below the snowline or else the snowfield was well *above* the location given and high on the mountain. (In August, the snowline was well above High Camp.) At any rate, I searched up the trail, then for some distance on the Round-The-Mountain Trail before returning to the base camp with no results.

When the helicopter arrived from King County, the fixed-wing aircraft was pulled from the search and the Huey continued. Late in the afternoon, word was received that one of the ground search parties had located the lost hiker and they requested a helicopter evacuation. They were in a forested area well below timberline and advised that the Huey would have to find a location for a landing zone to pick up the fellow. Then the fun began. The Huey came back to the base camp area and dropped off the approved CWMR searchers. The pilot asked where I was since this was in Yakima County. The base camp folks said I was around somewhere, but I was not State Certified to work with helicopters. The pilot explained that he was not that confident in the abilities of the CWMR folks he had in the helicopter and he wanted me because he had worked with me and knew what I could do.

"Deputy Steve" Sutliff of YSO drove up the road to the SAR van to get me and take me to the base LZ immediately. The Huey was approaching a low fuel state and would not be able to spend much more time on scene. When I arrived at the helicopter, the pilot and I took a moment to get reacquainted, then he loaded his Seattle crewmembers aboard along with me and my pack. We flew to the subject's location, then located a nearby swamp with low bushes and scattered trees where he could drop me about six feet from the skid into the swamp. I could then go to the location of the subject and prepare him for liftoff. There was no place to actually land, nor did the Huey have a hoist.

As the Huey flew over the location of the subject, the Crew Chief wrote a note and fastened it to a rock he had brought along. After fastening a piece of plastic flagging tape to the rock, he dropped it close to the folks on the ground. The note told them to have someone stand in a small clearing near there and indicate by holding his arms straight up if the subject could walk out or by holding his arms straight out from his shoulders if he needed to be carried. The ground party indicated the subject was able to walk and could go with them to the trail and walk out.

The response of the pilot was to fly back to the base LZ, offload me, and my pack, then depart for Seattle. The base camp folks started packing up. When the subject arrived with the last team to return to base, everyone departed for home.

❖ ❖ ❖

A 7 August 2004 callout of CWMR resulted in four of us departing for Mt. Adams. The wives of two fellows were in Portland, OR, and were rather apprehensive because their husbands had not returned from a climb of Mt. Adams. The two men were in their early seventies. They had climbed Mt. Adams at least twenty-five years before and now they had planned to do it again. They had moved to New Jersey at least that long ago and had lived there ever since. After moving to New Jersey, they had hiked in the local areas there, but had not gotten any high altitude experience in the intervening years.

A forest fire was burning south of the mountain, and the Forest Service had closed the road accessing the mountain. Apparently, the two climbers had gone in just before the road was closed. Climbers on the south side of Mt. Adams were able to return from the mountain, but access was closed to parties going in.

The climbers had planned on camping at the Lunch Counter (9,000 feet) and taking a couple of days to make the ascent, but they were at least a day overdue when their wives had reported them missing. Since only four CWMR members were available, YSO called Klickitat County for assistance from their SAR folks. Connie and I were two of the CWMR members who drove down in our vehicle, while Jeff Main and Powell McClean took the CWMR truck. We met with the Klickitat SAR folks at Trout Lake, and both teams went in together. The Forest Service escorted the party past the forest fire hazard area, then the teams drove to the road end at the Cold Springs campground. There the teams split up, the SAR folks searching several areas below the Round-The-Mountain Trail. The CWMR folks divided into two teams of two each and proceeded on separate routes up the south side of Mt. Adams looking for any trace of the climbers. Connie and I went up the trail on the rocks to the west of the south climb route while the other two were on the east side of the snowfield leading to the Lunch Counter.

At 9,000 feet the other team spotted a tent in a rock ring west of the regular route to the Lunch Counter, so all four of us headed for it. One fellow was outside the tent and when the team got to the site, he told us the body of his partner was in the tent. While Connie cooked some food for the survivor, we got the story of a climb gone wrong.

Due to the timing of their departure, the two fellows had driven to the road end, just missing the road closure by the Forest Service, but no one else was climbing up the south side that late in the day. They saw a few climbers going down as they went up, but that had not raised any concerns. It was normal. They spent their first night on the mountain at 9,000 feet in their tent just below the Lunch Counter. They got up early the next morning and started up the mountain. At some point between the Lunch Counter and the top, the other climber had commented that he felt rather weak, so the two of them returned to the tent, planning to complete the climb the next day. During that night, a storm left a deposit of rime ice on the windward side of the rock shelter around the tent.

The next morning, neither was too enthusiastic about continuing the climb, but they got dressed and the survivor cooked their breakfast while his partner lay down to rest a bit more. When breakfast was ready, the survivor went into the tent to tell his partner and found him comatose. He was unable to rouse him; his breathing was shallow and ragged. Shortly after that, he completely stopped breathing.

The climbers' tent just below the Lunch Counter (looking north). Jeff Main in the blue shirt and Powell McClean with orange pants. The survivor is wearing the red hat, and Connie Buchanan is cooking breakfast for the survivor.

The survivor then found himself stuck on the mountain. He couldn't remember exactly how they had reached the place where they put the tent up and then he discovered that unlike any normal day on the south side, no other climbers were around. He didn't want to leave his partner, nor did he want to start down without knowing the location of the trail to the campsite. One thing he did remember was an old rule: "If you don't know where you are, DO NOT move away from the spot where you are." His partner was dressed and in his sleeping bag, so the survivor wandered around the area looking for the trail without losing sight of the tent. He ate the last of their food that day, watching for other climbers. There were none. The next day he continued watching for climbers and spotted the CWMR teams climbing up Mt. Adams toward him.

Getting ready to leave.
Note the clouds blowing in from the west.

When we reached his campsite, Connie heated up some of our food for the survivor while the other three of us from CWMR wrapped the deceased climber in the ground cloth. After the survivor was fed and ready to go down, Connie led him back down the trail, both of them carrying the tent and some equipment. We cleaned up the campsite and started sliding the deceased climber down the snowfield toward the bottom of the mountain. The trip down alternated between towing the body on the flatter portions of the snowfield and belaying it down steep snow and patches of ice. Down toward the Crescent Glacier, some ice needed to be negotiated while easing the body down some rather steep snow slopes.

At one point, one of the team slipped and fell down a section of steep snow. All three of us were carrying heavy packs. With his large pack on, he was unable to get into an arrest position. He managed to get into a position where the pack was downhill from his body before he slammed into a large rock protruding from the snow. It was a sudden stop, but luckily he was not injured; the pack absorbed the impact. As we got down below the Crescent Glacier area, we met some of the SAR folks coming up.

Departure. Looking east. "Lunch Counter"
is on top of the ridge in the background.

The team was still on steep snow for a while, and some of the SAR members climbed up to help. It was at that time that one SAR fellow asked me to lend him my ice axe. He was stuck on some steep snow and was afraid to move. When asked, the fellow admitted he had no training with an axe but he "had read about" using one. I cut some bucket steps for the fellow to get over to the rocks where he could go back down the mountain. Then a sheriff's deputy (in uniform) admitted he was stuck also, so I chopped some steps in the snow for him.

The orange Cascade Litter (stretcher) is to the right of the center of the photo behind the fellow in the checkered shirt. The snow is colored by algae that live in the snow and are visible late in the year. This is supposed to be a "Wilderness Area," but note the cairn, center skyline, one of many the Forest Service built to mark the route.

The SAR folks brought a litter up to the edge of the snow-field. We loaded the body into it then carried it to Cold Springs, the road end. My diagnosis was that the climber's death was a case of "High Altitude Pulmonary Edema," but the subject's wife said he had some heart problems, so the Yakima County Coroner ruled that was the cause of death. There was no autopsy. Since the family was in Portland, the Yakima County Coroner released the body to them from Cold Springs and it was transported to Portland.

Early one hunting season, a report came to the Yakima County Sheriff's Office that a hunter had found some human bones and a rifle near a tree north of Fife's Peaks. CWMR was called out and hiked into the area on foot. The description of the scene was very explicit and when we got there, a round white ball could easily be seen from the trail. When we went to the spot, we found that the white ball was the weathered skull of a young man, probably in his teens or earlier. The scattered bones were gathered up, put in a plastic bag, and carried out in the pack of one of the CWMR members, while another member carried the slightly rusty rifle. It had been about a five-mile hike to the scene, a short time examining the area and gathering the remains, then five more miles hiking out in warm, sunny weather. That was not the usual weather for a mission.

It was later determined that the remains were of a young fellow who had disappeared while hunting a few years before. He had gone missing in bad weather and his reported hunting location was several miles away in another river valley. The search for him had been carried out where he had said he was going, rather than where he actually was. This was another example of not leaving an accurate location for searchers to look when a hunter comes up missing.

❖ ❖ ❖

The last mission for Connie and me was on 23 July 2009 when YSO called us to help search for two missing Boy Scouts. The scouts were missing after a hike out of Camp Fife, the Boy Scout camp in Yakima County. When we arrived at the search base, we were directed to a trail a short distance from Camp Fife. We had hiked a mile or so up the trail when we were called on the radio and told to return to the search base. The scouts had contacted a relative in Yakima via cell phone and were OK. They did not know where they were, but after some conversations with the SAR coordinator and the fact that they had found a road near the ridge's top, searchers had a possible location. We left the search base in our 4 x 4 pickup and drove to Dry Creek Road, out of the Nile area, and followed the road to its end near the ridge's top. Upon arriving, we found that a Jeep with its SAR driver was there helping the scouts put out the fire they had built on the road. The Jeep driver was going to take them back to Camp Fife. After discussing it on the radio with the search coordinator, we started home. En route, back down Dry Creek Road, we met another vehicle with some CWMR folks who were arriving on the scene. After passing on the word to return, both vehicles met at the Woodshed Restaurant to compare notes, then we returned to Yakima. This last mission of eleven hours and 151 miles of driving time topped off well over 25,000 miles of personal vehicle travel and over 3,100 hours of time logged on missions for various sheriffs.

With no mission callouts after that in 2009, Connie and I sent Sheriff Irwin our retirement letters effective 31 December 2009, ending fifty-eight years in the field for me and eighteen for Connie. We received handshakes and many thanks from Sheriff Irwin.

CHAPTER 5

EMT AND IV TECH

SEATTLE MOUNTAIN RESCUE HAD a program in the 1960s where some of their first aid members would work at Harborview Hospital on a voluntary basis to keep their skills current and stay familiar with handling seriously injured persons. This was organized by the Medical Director of MRC, Doctor Otto Trott. As EMT training came into being, those members took that advanced training also. I had heard of this program at Seattle MRC board meetings and asked a couple of the Emergency Department doctors in Yakima if they would start such a program. Memorial Hospital agreed to work with CWMR, and I first participated in the program, with Judy Beehler and later Clint Crocker following. All three of us were on the White Pass Ski Patrol with considerable first aid training as well as being members of CWMR.

The training program started when the Emergency Department at Memorial was in a few small rooms at the east end of the hospital and continued after their move to the west end of the hospital. The head nurse was a stickler for getting things done right, but she seemed to have a soft spot for us younger volunteers who were there to get some skills beyond the usual first aid. She knew that we wanted to work more at ease with injured persons in the field, patients who were often a long distance from conventional medical assistance.

In those days, no one except the surgeons (and perhaps not them) wore gloves when working with patients. The EMTs washed their hands a lot, both before and after working on each patient, but no one was concerned about many of the things people would worry about ten years later.

The old Emergency Department in Memorial Hospital consisted of three or four rooms on the east side of the hospital. One night we had a patient who had seriously injured himself trying to commit suicide. He kept saying he wanted a knife so he could finish the job, but the staff had him restrained on the gurney so the doctor could stitch his wounds. A nurse saw a psychiatrist going down the hall and intercepted him. It was after 2200 hours and everyone was getting tired. She told him the problem; the doctor asked the patient's name. When she told him, the doctor said that was a patient of his. He said he was getting tired of that patient's constant suicide attempts, but went in and listened to the patient's story, which he told the staff was just a continuation of his attempts to get others to feel sorry for him. After his wounds were stitched up, he was transferred to the fifth floor: the psychiatric floor of Memorial Hospital.

No one kept the statistics, but there was quite a feeling that there were more injuries (and particularly psychiatric problems) when the moon was full than on other nights. In fact, if it was a very busy night in the ER, someone could be counted on to ask if the moon was full or not. Often it was a full moon.

Another night, a fellow was brought in by ambulance with a bullet hole through his thigh. A state trooper had seen him trying to thumb a ride somewhere west of Ellensburg so stopped and picked him up. All went well until the trooper stopped in Ellensburg to let him out. The hitchhiker grabbed the trooper and tried to stab him with a knife. The trooper was backing out of his side of the car with the assailant holding on to him and swinging the knife, which, fortunately, was not very sharp. As the trooper got out of the car with the fellow hanging on, a passerby pulled the .357 revolver from the trooper's holster, put it against the assailant's thigh, and pulled the trigger. That stopped the fight.

The assailant was taken to the Ellensburg Hospital, given emergency treatment, and transferred to Yakima. When he arrived at Memorial Hospital, the patient had a gag covering his mouth and was secured to the gurney. When the ER doctor saw the patient, he told the nurse to take the gag off. The ambulance fellows told the doctor, "He spits!" The doctor repeated his instructions, so the nurse complied. The patient promptly spit right into the doctor's face. The doctor turned around, told the nurse to put a towel over the patient's face, then washed his own face. He followed that by ordering a syringe and a tranquilizing medication, administered it, and then started working on the injury (which included a fractured femur).

The patient was kept in the hospital for a long time at taxpayers' expense then tried in court for assaulting the officer. The defense got him released saying that he was disoriented in Ellensburg, was suffering a mental problem, and in the end, he was released and given transportation to his home in California. A few months after he got there, we read in the newspaper that he was wanted in California for a crime. After holding his mother hostage in the family home and shooting at someone who was walking up to the house the SWAT team there fired a "flash-bang" into the house, accidently setting it on fire. When the individual came running out of the house shooting a rifle, a police sniper shot and killed him, then the officers released his mother, and the fire department put out the fire.

In those days, the ER rooms in both hospitals in Yakima were staffed by nurses. If a doctor was needed, the doctors maintained a rotating list of "on-call" doctors who could be called to work on seriously injured or ill patients. As there began to be more patients coming into the emergency rooms of both hospitals, they modified the Emergency Departments and staffed each with a team of doctors that confined their practice to only emergency work. That later became a specialty practice for which medical schools trained doctors.

As the new ER was developed in Memorial Hospital, it was moved into the west end of the building. One night in the new ER rooms, the ambulance brought in a soldier who had been bitten by a rattlesnake at the Yakima Firing Center. He had shoved a blank round into each end of his rifle and shot the snake, using the blank in the muzzle as the projectile. The snake was a very large rattler, which he brought with him as proof that it was a rattlesnake. He left the snake in a plastic bag on the floor of the exam room and when the patient was taken to a floor for observation, someone asked, "What happened to the snake?" It was gone, leaving some minor panic in its wake until it was noticed that the plastic bag was also missing. Most snakes do not carry plastic bags with them as they leave.

A short time later, the x-ray technician came into the ER and hung a couple of x-ray negatives on the light box. The x-rays were of a large rattlesnake, coiled on the table. Visible were the remains of seven sage rats inside the snake. The most recent was a complete skeleton and the oldest was just a collection of teeth.

After several years volunteering at Memorial, I then spent ten years as a volunteer in the Emergency Department at St. Elizabeth's Hospital. Both hospitals had a volunteer program, but the CWMR volunteers were outside those programs. The staff members who ran the volunteer program did not know the CWMR volunteers were working there.

When the criteria to teach an Emergency Medical Technician course was finalized by a committee of doctors, I was planning on going to Seattle twice a week to attend an EMT class. Then one was set up in Yakima by James T. "Jim" Dodge, MD, who was the first certified EMT instructor for Yakima County. The class, however, was limited to police, fire, and ambulance personnel. The number of students was limited and the class was full. Clint Crocker, Judy Beehler, and I wanted to take the class. All of us were on the Ski Patrol at White Pass Ski Area and knew Jim quite well since he was also the Medical Advisor for the White Pass Ski Patrol. We pleaded with him—it would be a real strain to go to Seattle two nights a week, and there were no excuses for missing even one class. He gave in; he would like to have some EMTs on the ski patrol. He told us just to attend the classes. He was sure some of the officers or firemen would drop out after the first couple of classes and he could put the names of the CWMR members in place of those who dropped out. He was right. All three of us got our EMT certification.

The switch from Memorial Hospital to Saint Elizabeth's Hospital started with a mountain rescue mission to rescue a seriously injured elk hunter in November of 1975. He had been riding his horse when he and the horse came through some heavy brush and found themselves head to head with a small herd of elk. Both the elk herd and the horse reversed directions suddenly. The horse threw the rider off but trapped one of his feet in the stirrup for a short distance. His injuries included a broken pelvis and a couple of broken bones in his leg. His hunting companion rode several miles for help, and Central Washington Mountain Rescue was called in. For this night mission, the fresh snow was above our knees, but the brush and trees were so thick that snowshoes were of little value. We carried a Cascade Litter (similar to a Stokes litter, but it was a fiberglass sled and built in two pieces for ease in carrying to the scene, see page 148) put it together, administered first aid, then dragged him in the sled out to the highway to a waiting ambulance.

The later critique from the doctors pointed out that he had serious internal bleeding and CWMR should have administered an IV. There were no such skills in the unit. Dr. Olson volunteered to teach some of us the technique if we would keep up our skills by constant practice in the hospital. Four volunteered to take the instruction. Clint Crocker, Judy Beehler, Brian Zeutenhorst, and I participated in the program, volunteering in the Emergency Department one evening each week. By the time we were finished with the class and doing IVs on practice arms, just like the nurses in training did, the three who had stayed in the program had to take a final exam. After we all passed the written test, we had to take turns doing an IV on each other. The student who put the IV in my arm was nervous (as was I), and when the student wiped my arm with the alcohol swab, the alcohol was still in a puddle there when the sixteen-gauge needle was inserted through the alcohol and the skin. That was very interesting (as in, PAINFUL), and led the instructor to point out that the alcohol should dry first! All of us passed that test. We were then taught how to administer three different drugs in the field. We could pick up the materials for the IVs and the meds we were to inject from the hospital before leaving on a mission and were to be in radio contact with the ER doctor, who would then authorize the administration of whatever he felt was necessary.

A committee was working statewide with the various ambulance services to bring them to a state standard. Many decisions had to be made before the doctors on the committee would decide what skills ambulance personnel had to have before they were certified to work. At that time, anyone with a panel truck could advertise as an ambulance service, and a couple of garages in the lower valley did so. One of them had a reputation for bringing patients in during the day with grease from the mechanic's hands on the patient. Most funeral homes in the bigger towns and cities also had a hearse that could be pressed into service to haul injured persons to the hospital, as well as take the dead folks to their mortuary. Requiring an ambulance to be a specialized vehicle and to have specially trained personnel on each trip met much resistance, but it did come to pass. From that came today's specialized ambulance services.

Dr. Olson's next hurdle was to convince the committee he had some IV therapy students who were volunteer EMT folks and the IV training was necessary for patient care in the mountains. At an emergency medicine conference in Yakima about the same time, there was a lot of discussion about who should be allowed to administer IVs and drugs. The Seattle doctor, chairman of the committee, was rather adamant about not allowing volunteers to do so. The paramedic program was just getting started for ambulance providers. The Yakima doctors pointed out that a lot of remote mountain terrain is unreachable by ambulance. (At that time, helicopters were not being used for medical evacuations very often.) As a result of the discussions between the doctors and ambulance providers, CWMR continued providing IV therapy on a volunteer basis. The medical personnel required Central Washington Mountain Rescue personnel to complete some rather stringent competency testing and maintain regular practice to get and keep their licenses as Intravenous Therapy Technicians.

The first card of many.

Each one had to administer at least nine IVs every ninety days, and some small amount of drug injections were required. All three of the CWMR members were working in the St. Elizabeth ER at that point. I was the only one who kept in practice over the long haul. That was done by working in the Emergency Department at St. Elizabeth's Hospital one night almost every week and spending a few additional mornings working with the hospital's IV team. The night shifts were six hours long, so I put in well over 2,000 hours in my ten years of volunteering in St. Elizabeth Hospital.

Because of the time required to stay current, the other two dropped from the program, but I continued volunteering in the ER and was volunteering with the IV nurse team on the floors in St. Elizabeth's Hospital on some occasions. One morning I was asked in private by each of the IV nurses on duty if I would be comfortable doing an IV on the senior IV nurse who was going in for surgery that morning. I had no qualms about that and told them so. When I went into the senior IV nurse's room, she told me that all three of the nurses had asked her if she was comfortable with me doing her IV that morning. She said she had trained me and felt I would be able to handle it well. The IV needle was a number twelve, bigger than any I had ever used, and her arm was really slender. Her veins were big enough, so I proceeded. As I was putting on a dressing to stabilize the cannula after it was inserted, I looked over my shoulder and all three of the IV nurses were watching. I asked, "Is this a final exam or something?" The IV was a success and had been quite easy. They all laughed and left. That was when my patient said, "They were 'chicken!'" (She was known as a hard-driving taskmaster.)

After a year or two, the permission for CWMR to administer drugs was withdrawn. We had used that training only once in the field, on a mission to Klootchman Rock that is described on page 128. I did only three IVs in the field in ten years, but they were all in rather difficult circumstances. They all worked, but one took three sticks in really cold winter weather. All total, I did about three hundred IVs in the hospital. On one IV that I was asked to do, the nurse told me that the patient was a drug addict and probably didn't have any good veins, but I could look. If I couldn't find one, she would call for an IV nurse. I found one right away, on his forearm where the patient had a big tattoo of a skull. I came out of the patient's room quite soon, and the nurse started to call IV Therapy to get an expert on the job. I told her the IV was in. She was baffled. I was a volunteer but had done the job so fast. She asked where I put it. My response really shook her up: "In the left eye socket!" Then I told her about the tattoo and she had to see for herself.

About a year later, another nurse sent me in to do an IV and told me it was a druggie who probably had no veins left. It was the same fellow. I asked the patient if he had saved the vein I had used a year before. The patient was pretty groggy, but looked at me, smiled, and said yes. Sure enough the vein was still good and I was back out at the desk in a few minutes. "Where?" she asked. "Left eye socket!" I said, grinning. It caused another shocked nurse, who was on her way to the patient's room before I could tell her about the tattoo!

It is hard to believe now, but in those days, the used needles were put into a thin cardboard box, called a "sharps box," after use and then specially disposed of. The box had a round hole in the top made by cutting three lines across each other, making an asterisk of cuts, then pushing the pie-shaped wedges down into the box. One night I dropped an IV needle into the "sharps" box after completing an IV. It snagged on the pie-shaped cardboard cutout and bounced back up, stabbing me in the back of the hand. It was a minor injury, but according to protocol, I reported it to the head nurse. Her first remark was that I had better hope I didn't catch what the patient was in there for! Another nurse laughed and said the patient was pregnant. This was followed by some discussion by the ladies about who was going to get to give me the shot in my rear with the antibiotic—all five ccs of it! They even talked about making more than one shot. The one male nurse in the ER listened to all the discussion, laughed, and said, "Come on, Lynn, I'll do it!"

After working more than six hours a night, one night a week for ten years, the protocols were getting rather tight as more requirements came in for handling patients. The nurses had to take more and more training and concern increased regarding a volunteer being in the Emergency Department. I was getting more involved in other volunteer projects with constant demands for my time by then, so reluctantly I gave up my IV Technician classification and quit working as a volunteer in the Emergency Department.

CHAPTER 6

MOUNTAIN RESCUE ASSOCIATION

*The emblem of the national Mountain Rescue Association,
affixed to a Seattle Mountain Rescue (SMR) jacket.*

The national Mountain Rescue Association (MRA) was orga-nized at a meeting of local teams from several of the western states at Mt. Hood in the summer of 1959. The history of MRA is covered in a book written by Dee Molenaar and published in 2009 for the fiftieth anniversary meeting at Mt. Hood. The book is titled *Mountains Don't Care, But We Do* and is available at The Mountaineers Bookstore and other bookstores. Each of the Washington units is featured with a page or two in the book, as is the story of the formation of the Washington Mountain Rescue Association. Another section, "Selected Mountain Rescue Leadership in Washington," features many of the early Mountain Rescue leaders, as well as six of the early leaders from the Yakima area. They are Dave Mahre, Bill and Gene Prater, Bob McCall, Judy Hanna, and me. In addition to that book, there is a DVD of the same name by Rick Lorenz (Topograph Media) with interviews of eight of the early leaders from Washington and Oregon. They were Dick Pooley (Crag Rats), Dee Molenaar (MRC), Jim Whittaker (MRC), Wolf Bauer (MRC), George Sainsbury (MRC), Fran Sharp (TMRU), Rocky Henderson (Portland), and me (CWMR). This DVD also can be purchased from The Mountaineers Bookstore as well as many other bookstores. Also, most public libraries have copies of each book and DVD.

I started attending MRA meetings sometime in the early to mid-1960s and have attended most of them since that time. They are a great way to practice new techniques of rescue and rehash old rescues.

For many years, MRA held two regular meetings each year, starting with summer meetings held over Father's Day weekend and fall meetings on Thanksgiving weekend. On occasion there would be an additional meeting for some special purpose. At first, the meetings were scheduled so that the summer meet-ings were sponsored by MRA units in the northern states and held there. The fall meetings were held in the southern states.

They were primarily outdoor training sessions with a few indoor meetings and the annual elections. Gradually, that schedule changed to the point that the summer meetings (the major meetings of the year) are now held without consideration for the weather and location but are still usually scheduled near Father's Day weekend. The fall meetings have been moved to the wintertime and have been held at Salt Lake City, Utah, in mid-January for the last several years. This usually provides time for some attendees to get in a few days of skiing before or after the weekend meeting. These meetings involve concentrated indoor planning and organizational discussions with no outdoor training sessions.

In June of 1974 at the annual summer meeting of the MRA, several members of Seattle MRC approached me. They wanted to nominate me to be the President of MRA. The existing slate of prospective officers was not looked on with total enthusiasm by some of the region's personnel, and they said they needed someone who could get things straightened out without further ruffling the feathers of the regions that were unhappy. I agreed and at the election found myself not only nominated, but also elected almost unanimously. Among other things, there had been problems with annual reports (financial and others) not getting in on time and that was accomplished during my term, not without some acrimony, but it was accomplished.

In November 1974, the national Mountain Rescue Association (MRA) conference was held in Sacramento, CA. This was the first fall meeting after I was elected President. The Air Force sent quite a delegation to demonstrate how they operated on rescue missions. The Commanding General from Scott Air

Force Base attended with them. The general's co-pilot was an officer from Toppenish, WA, Dale Stovall, who had been my mentor at the Air Force Academy on my first Active Duty tour there many years before. He told me that he had asked for the trip to Sacramento, thinking I might be there. The Air Force had a large demonstration on Saturday. They brought some "Jolly Green" helicopters and showed the way they were used as well as demonstrating refueling in flight and dropping parachutists to aid the injured on the ground. The general expected to fully participate in the evening dinner on Saturday, so Dale had to plan on being the pilot flying back to Scott AFB in the early morning hours Sunday. The general could party late with the mountain rescue folks but not Dale because of the "eight hours from bottle to throttle" rule.

This was the meeting where John Sebastian asked me to keep his billfold in my pocket because he was expecting to be involved in some horseplay after the dinner and expected to get thrown into the swimming pool. Sure enough, after dinner, one of the state employees from Olympia, WA, said something about how Judy Beehler should be tossed into the swimming pool. She foolishly replied, "You wouldn't dare." Moments later, he threw her—in her long dress—over his shoulder, carried her almost a block, and tossed her into the pool. Then the fun began. The fellow from Olympia landed in the pool, joined shortly after by a couple more fellows who were participating in the shenanigans. I, a sober fellow, was watching from the perimeter when several fellows jumped me from behind and carried me to the pool. On the way to the pool, I thought of *my* billfold and threw it to the ground. John's billfold stayed in the jacket pocket where it had been placed and landed in the pool with me. The horseplay ended with a sheriff's deputy walking along the edge of the pool with a smile on his face enjoying the fun, but it put a stop to the activity.

Several of us from the CWMR delegation were staying in one room and it really became a humid place with all the wet clothing dripping on the floor Saturday night.

The next morning, the deputy was having breakfast in the motel dining room when some of the MRA folks walked in. He commented on the fun and games the night before. Furthermore, he said that he felt he had made a mistake walking along the edge of the pool to calm things down. At the time he had the feeling there might have been a thought to accidently bump him also. Several of the MRA folks commented that the same thought had occurred to them.

The following summer, 1975, I was presiding as MRA President and the master of ceremonies at a joint US-Canada Mountain Rescue Conference in Vancouver, BC. This was also the regular June meeting of the MRA. I flew to Seattle in my airplane to pick up a couple of the members of Seattle MRC who were also going to attend the conference. George Sainsbury was one of them, and the other (who shall remain nameless) really looked like a "hippy" in those days. He attracted the attention of the Canadian Immigration folks, and I (as the pilot bringing him into Canada) was called aside and asked to sign some documents attesting to my responsibility to escort that Seattle member and to be responsible for taking him back to the United States when the conference was over.

The main speaker for the dinner at the Annual Meeting was a member of the British Columbia Legislature and a pilot for one of the two major Canadian airlines at the time. In the table talk during the dinner, he told how Canada had a problem with the language difficulty in Quebec. The French-speaking people in Quebec were pushing to make French the national language in spite of the majority of English-speaking people in Canada. He told how the folks in Quebec called their language French, but he flew from Vancouver to Montreal to Paris and each city had its own language. Montreal and Paris did not have the same language—close, but not the same.

A highlight that occurred during my term of office as National President of MRA was an invitation to me by the US Federal Government to address a joint US-NATO Conference in May of 1976 on Specialized Rescue. My paper titled "Special Rescue Operations under Difficult Environmental Conditions" was published in the *Collected Papers* after the conference. The conference included fifteen nations and the International Red Cross and was held in Baltimore, Maryland. The conference was very interesting, as were the various presentations by EMS, police, and fire rescue teams of the city and county around Baltimore.

Connie and I had resigned from CWMR in December of 2009, but Seattle SMR then voted me in as an Honorary Member of SMR based on my history of working with SMR for more than fifty-eight years and my active participation with them on big missions. In 2010, the Spring Conference was held in Juneau, Alaska. We (Connie and I) flew to Juneau to attend the conference. We visited with many of our old friends and participated in some of the seminars, even though we were no longer active. At the Annual Meeting and dinner, both Connie and I were called up front and given citations honoring our years of active participation in the field on searches and on rescues.

Connie Buchanan receiving her eighteen-year certificate from Dan Hourihan, MRA Past President, at the national MRA conference in Juneau, AK, 2010.

Lynn receiving his fifty-eight-year certificate from Tim Cochrane, Past MRA President, at the national MRA conference in Juneau, AK, 2010. Lynn Buchanan in the red sweater, Tim Kovaks, Past MRA President, on Lynn's left; on Tim's left is Monty Bell Past MRA President; behind the fellow taking a picture is Fran Sharp, Past MRA President; last, in the black cap, is Rocky Henderson, Past MRA President.
Photo by Connie Buchanan.

Tim Cochrane, Past MRA President, reading the citation accompanying the award to Lynn Buchanan at the national MRA conference in Juneau, AK, 2010.

The last speech by Buchanan. Dan Hourihan, Past MRA President MRA, far left. Rick Lorenz is seated to his left and almost behind the post. Photos by Connie Buchanan.

The
Mountain
Rescue
Association

Connie Buchanan

Central Washington Mountain Rescue
Distinguished Service
1991 - 2009

JUNE 18, 2010

President

Dan Hourihan
Awards Chairman
Mountain Rescue Association

Dan,

I am writing today to nominate Lynn Buchanan, Past President of the MRA, Founding member of the Central Washington MRA Team, former member of Seattle Mtn Rescue.

Lynn, over the years has distinguished himself not only in the field, but consistently has attended National meetings and served as an MRA officer in too many positions to list. He is one of only two Past Presidents, which served a 3 year term as President.

From my first meeting in 1982, to present I cannot remember Lynn not being there. His keen sense of MRA Traditions guides us as we look to the future while remembering our past.
The story goes that OME DIABER, founding father asked Lynn to join Seattle and that started a 58 year affair with MRA. Yes starting in 1952, (I was 2 yo), until today Lynn Buchanan, has provided a life time of service to our organization.

In summary, Lynn not only deserves our recognition for a lifetime of service, he earned it the old fashion way, In THE FIELD, stepping up through his region, and then on to being a National officer

On behalf of the Past Presidents' of the MRA, I respectfully nominate Lynn Buchanan for the MRA Life time of Service award.

Tim Cochrane,
Past President 95-98
Mountain Rescue Association

The Mountain Rescue Association

Lynn Buchanan

**Lifetime Service
1952 - 2009**

6/18/10

President

Many of the MRA conferences attended by me have been chronicled and, with the photos taken by me, were rare adventures. They may be printed later.

ADDENDUM

WHAT FOLLOWS ARE SEVERAL stories by Lex Maxwell, Lynn Buchanan and others in Central Washington Mountain Rescue (CWMR), a copy of the *Iceworm* (a short-term, occasional newsletter with stories of some of CWMR's missions) and another, more recent story or two.

CWMR HISTORY
by Lex Maxwell
(circa 1999)

The history of Mountain Rescue for the Yakima area seems so prosaic when reduced to dates, people, and statistics. The real story lies in the courage, stamina, skill, dedication, and comradeship of those who participated; and in the tragedies, both with happy and unhappy endings, which were the occasions of rescue. A fascinating book could be written from this material.

The idea of a rescue unit came about at the urging of my old friend, Ome Daiber, who with Wolf Bauer and others started the Mountain Rescue Council of Seattle. They often came into the East Cascades and wanted help from some of us local climbers. This was about twenty-eight years ago. I was up to my neck in many other activities but managed to call together a number of climbing and ski patrol friends to discuss the possibility of forming an organization.

Louis G. Newhall, an ardent National Ski patrolman, agreed to accept the chairmanship of our embryo group. He was a very dedicated leader and would drive all night to attend rescue meetings in Seattle to bring us information and share experiences with their council.

Our early needs were manifold. We had to train our personnel in techniques of evacuation for injured people, in first aid training, in teamwork, and how to cooperate with the civil authorities as well as other rescue units. We needed money to buy berg tragas, litters, ropes, first aid supplies, climbing equipment, and radios. We raised the money, we trained our people, and it was long, hard, and sometimes thankless. Yet along the way, a call for help would come and as everything cranked into gear, it gave a new stimulus to our efforts. Publicity in the media was helpful because it mentioned names of those involved.

We had an asset in personnel with Marcel Schuster who had been in the Berg Watch, which is a group of mountain guides in Germany who could be called in for rescue. Later, he served throughout WWII in the German mountain troops. Some of the training he was able to pass on to us in rescue techniques was invaluable.

In addition to Louis Newhall and me, early presidents of our mountain rescue unit were Bob McCall, Hal Foss, Gene Prater, and Lynn Buchanan.

One of the first things we did was to develop a procedure manual that each member kept near his telephone; we also furnished copies to the Sheriffs' offices and the Forest Service offices. Another big step was to get similar rescue units established in Ellensburg and Wenatchee, as well as in Dr. Don Fager of Wenatchee giving leadership to these units.

During the early years, we developed some complex arrangements with Civil Defense, with the radio hams, and with other organizations who could assist us. The radio "ham" groups were trained in communications, had the equipment, and formed an excellent statewide setup on many rescues. Civil Defense had staff, equipment, and offered us disability protection in case of accident.

However, there was always the haunting fear of a lawsuit being thrown at us for the liability of a mistake or negligence. So at one of our meetings with the Rescue Council, I discussed this with Paul Williams, a Seattle lawyer, who at that time was chairman of the Seattle unit. He recommended that we affiliate with the Rescue Council and by becoming a branch of the Council, we would enjoy the corporate shelter it had. We agreed. Paul worked out the needed resolution, and we became the Central Washington Unit of the Mountain Rescue Council.

Thereafter, one of us would always be a member of their board of directors. After a few years, I grew tired of driving back and forth to Seattle, so Lynn Buchanan agreed to serve. Lynn later not only became chairman of the Rescue Association, but went on to become chairman of the Mountain Rescue Association, a national organization of the Mountain Rescue units.

There is a lot more that should be recorded here, including the names of a lot of fine people whose work and dedication made the Central Washington unit of the Mountain Rescue Council an important and necessary organization for the humanity it serves. I am proud to have had a part in it.

— LEX MAXWELL

Deceased Members:

John Adams	Hal Foss	Barry Prather
Val Bedard	Jim Griffen	Joe Roemer
Merril Belton	Ed Link	Pat Sutphen
Jim Carlson	Chuck Lyons	Louie Ulrich
Jamie Christensen		Gene Prater

Past Members:

Lex Maxwell	
Judy (Beehler) Hanna	Wally Juneau
Jim Bjorgen	Matt Kerns
Tom Bjorgen	Jim Linse
Dick Blair	Phil Lizee
Paul Bourden	Tom Lyons
Walt Braton	Richard Lukins
Lynn Buchanan	Dave Mahre
Terry Burger	Gerald Marsh
Bill Butt	Bob McCall
Harry Caperton	Jim Obert
Clint Crocker	Dr. George Roulston
Dave Davidson	Jerry Schlesinger
Al Drengson	Kathy Schneider
Roger Durmont	John Sebastian
Craig Eilers	Paul Smith
Allan Ewert	Bob Swenson
Norm Ferguson	Bob Sutphen
Gary Foulkes	Dr. Clark Thompson
Ron Gelderman	Dave Thompson
Dallas Hake	John Thompson Sr.
Tom Hargis	John Thompson
Lee Henkle	Dr. Ralph Uber
Steve Hoit	Hank Weber
Gary Holscher	Dorothy Wood
Don Jones	Brian Zeutenhorst

Ellensburg Unit:

Gene Prater	Bill Prater	Barry Prather
Fred Stanley	Fred Dunham	

(By 2013, many on the later list have also passed on. Wonderful folks! – Lynn B.)

❖ ❖ ❖

MT ADAMS RESCUE
31 JUNE 57

When four climbers of a six-member team failed to return to base camp by nightfall, Sunday, June 30, 1957, large contingents of Mountain Rescue members from Yakima, Ellensburg, Goldendale, Longview, Seattle, and Hood River converged at the foot of the Mt. Adams Icefall the next morning to begin the search for the missing.

As search efforts were getting underway, two of the climbers, Dr. Ralph Uber and Bob Swenson, arrived back at base camp, reporting that the other two were uninjured but were stranded on a ledge located on the west flank of the Icefall. The search was called off, and it was decided that only two rescuers, Gene Prater of Ellensburg and Marcel Schuster of Yakima, were needed to climb the snowfield west of the Icefall and lead the stranded climbers from the ledge back to base camp—a task accomplished without further difficulty.

The scenario that led to the failed climb began when two members of the team, Bob McCall and Don Jones, left base camp at 2:00 a.m., ahead of the rest, to begin pioneering a route through the jumble of seracs and crevasses that constitute the Adams Icefall. McCall and Jones expected the other four members would soon catch up.

However, their expectations never materialized, the anticipated rendezvous never occurred. After stalling and waiting until near midday, McCall and Jones abandoned the climb, returning to base camp via the northwest ridge to discover the fate of the other four. With darkness approaching and still no trace of the missing climbers, the fear that the missing teams had met with a serious accident was clear. George Gans, who was in support at High Camp, was sent back to Yakima to call for additional help. In anticipation of a technical rescue in the Icefall, word was spread to most of the regional MRA units, resulting in one of the greater gatherings of rescuers in the northwest.

The lesson to be learned: rope teams should never separate beyond the sight or sound of each other. The first mistake occurred when McCall and Jones left camp ahead of the rest. The other four climbers—Dr. Uber, Bob Swenson, Mike McGuire, and Dave Bishop—were experienced climbers, but they had never led before and found the Icefall beyond their leadership ability. Their difficulties were compounded when they attempted to exit the Icefall by climbing a steep rock slab covered with treacherous verglas. After spending hours on the slab, the rope team of McGuire and Bishop managed to reach a ledge, where they spent the night to await rescue.

The rope team of Uber and Swenson encountered even greater difficulty when Uber slipped on the verglas, breaking his ice axe. Despite his precarious position, Swenson's belay arrested Uber's fall. After recovering from this mishap, Uber and Swenson continued up the mountain, becoming benighted when darkness and fierce winds made movement hazardous. Not until 8:00 a.m. were they able to return to base camp. Fortunately no one suffered serious frostbite or injury.

– Bob McCall

GOOSE EGG
1967

The day was Sunday, April 17, 1967. For the middle of April, it was a wet, miserable day. With Dave Mahre leading, the rope team of Mahre and Bob McCall gently tapped pitons into the shallow indentations on the rock face of Goose Egg Mountain, near the Tieton reservoir. The pitons were more for psychological effect than physical safety, for the brittle rock on Goose Egg will not hold a properly driven piton.

The team's objective was to rescue seventeen-year-old Daniel Jackson, trapped on a steep rock face overlaid with patches of wet moss, ice, and snow. The climb would have been difficult for an expert under warm and dry conditions, but with darkness settling in and rain mixed with light snow flurries, both Mahre and McCall wondered how it had been possible for young Jackson to have reached his present precarious position without falling. Of immediate concern was the awareness that conditions were worsening, the slope was becoming more hazardous, and McCall was of the opinion that Dave would be unable to reach Jackson without a slip or fall—in which case McCall would be unable to arrest Dave's fall, due to the absence of a decent foothold from which to set a rope belay.

To this day, McCall marvels at Dave's ability to reach Daniel Jackson in the rain, snow, and darkness, and then lower him by rope one hundred feet down the slope with no more to stand on than wet moss, lichen, and an occasional indentation in the rock.

Jackson had been climbing with another youngster, Calvin Winters, when Jackson became stranded. Winters was able to descend and go for help, notifying personnel at the Tieton ranger station, who, in turn, called the Central Washington Mountain Rescue Unit.

The day may have been wet and cold, but observing Dave Mahre perform the impossible, saving a young man's life, left this writer with a very warm feeling on that cold day and very proud to be a part of the Central Washington Mountain Rescue Unit.

ROBERT MCCALL
1218 S. 14TH AVE.
YAKIMA, WA 98902

❖ ❖ ❖

MT. LADY WASHINGTON, CO

On 16 June 1979 after the National Mountain Rescue Conference at Estes Park in Rocky Mountain National Park, Colorado, four of us from CWMR decided to take a day to do a bit of climbing in the park before returning to Yakima. We looked at climbing Longs Peak, but the locals told us that it was a two-day climb, and we didn't feel we had the time for that. So we settled on Mt. Lady Washington, 13,281 feet high, on the ridge above Chasm Lake. It was just a seven-mile hike on the trail into the Boulderfield on the north side of Longs Peak, with a short detour to the south and a climb up the east ridge of Lady Washington. After we reached the top, we felt we had a bit of time left before the afternoon thunderstorms would arrive, so we continued west to the Boulderfield and went up Longs Peak as far as the Keyhole. We then decided that we should be going down to stay ahead of the thunderstorms, but Longs would have been a one-day climb for us in the condition we were in, particularly after spending the time at altitude that we had spent at the MRA Conference in Estes Park.

The east face of Longs Peak from near Chasm Lake.
Lady Washington is to the right.

A couple of the subjects covered at the conference were high altitude injuries, including High Altitude Pulmonary Edema (HAPE), and High Altitude Cerebral Edema (HACE), both of which were common on Mt. Everest. Dr. Peter Hackett lectured on the subject. His clinic, located on the route in to Mt. Everest, had saved many lives at that altitude. After the lecture, some of us from Washington and Oregon had quite a chat with him, since we have a few volcanoes that reached into the altitudes he discussed in his lecture. This was the first time I met him, although we met again at a dinner in Seattle later when we were both at a Himalayan fund-raiser there. In Seattle when I introduced myself to him, he commented that he was sure we had met somewhere before. It had been there in Rocky Mountain National Park at the MRA Conference in 1979.

The team on the summit of Lady Washington, Colorado.
Steve in the red shirt, Judy in the blue jacket.

As the four of us, Steve Reese, Paul Smith, Judy Beehler, and me, were coming down through the Boulderfield at 12,600 feet elevation, we went past a tent at about 12,000 feet alongside the trail we were following to the ranger station. The ranger station was at 9,400 feet elevation at the end of the access road to Longs Peak. We still had about six miles or so to go to reach the ranger station. A fellow was lying on the ground at that tent, so we walked over to see if he was all right. It was strange to see someone lying down the way he was. He answered us, but he was totally confused about where he was or where his companions were. While we were talking to him, we concluded that we were dealing with a fellow who had the symptoms of HACE: mental confusion, slurring speech, and staggering as he tried to stand up or walk. He could not do either without help.

After a bit of conversation with him and learning that he didn't expect his companions back until "quite a bit later today," we decided among ourselves that we should attempt to walk him down to a lower altitude.

The north side of Longs Peak from the top of the Boulderfield.
There are climber tracks in the snow just below the
tiny tendril of cloud over the summit ridge.

He needed some help getting started, but he recognized that he was having a bit of trouble and that he had no idea how to get down the mountain. We helped him get some of his stuff together and into a pack, figuring that his companions could carry out the heavy stuff. We left a note for them telling them who we were and that we would leave their companion with the park rangers at the much lower altitude of the ranger station.

The first part of the trip was rather difficult getting him to stand up, staying on his feet with one of us on each side of him on the narrow trail, and getting him to walk or even talk coherently on the way down was even more difficult. We learned that he had left New Jersey (almost sea level) with a companion to climb Longs Peak. They flew into Denver (at approximately 5,000 feet elevation), got off the plane, rented a car, and drove to the ranger station at 9,700 feet, where they met a friend or two who knew the way in to Longs Peak. The three or four of them started hiking in as soon as they got together. They set up their tent where we had found the fellow and started the climb the next morning before daylight. The fellow with us said he had felt "really strange" when the others started out, so they left him at the tent to rest and they would rejoin him when they got back in the evening. After spending the night in the tent, they would come out the next day. We were pretty sure he would have been comatose or dead by the next morning, but his friends apparently did not know the seriousness of his condition.

He was more coherent when we got to the ranger station, but the rangers were concerned about his mental state. They had heard of HACE, but they had never seen anyone with the problem. After checking the fellow, they agreed with us and took over the care of him, telling us that they would get him back to Denver and medical attention as soon as a ride could be found, probably in an ambulance. They would pass the information on to his companions when they returned. They had signed out for the climb at the ranger station the day before. We got into our rental car and drove back to the airport where my Cherokee aircraft was waiting. After spending the night in Denver, we started the flight back to Yakima.

The snow-filled shelter on the north side of Longs Peak.
Photo by LKB.

❖ ❖ ❖

JUMP-OFF LOOKOUT ROAD
12 NOVEMBER 1979

Near the end of the hunting season in the area between the Rimrock "Y" and Rimrock Lake, darkness came early in the evening at that time of the year.

We were attending a CWMR meeting in the old Civil Defense rooms in the courthouse basement when a sheriff's deputy came in and announced that we were needed in the mountains just below Jump-Off Lookout. A van containing three hunters had driven off the road part of the way down the hill. One man was thrown or had jumped out just below the road. Another, supposedly pretty badly injured, was partway down the very steep hillside, and the third was near the bottom of the hill. The last one had been crushed by the vehicle and was dead. We were needed to pick up the injured one about halfway down the hill.

The first one had called for help from a passing motorist, who phoned the sheriff's office from the Rimrock "Y" (this was long before cell phones). YSO had called an ambulance, which was at the scene above where the vehicle had driven off the road. When we got to the highway bridge where the forest road went up the mountain, several of us were transported up to where the van had gone off the road. The ambulance was parked on the road at that point with a paramedic, whom I knew, standing by, waiting. He had some IV equipment wrapped in a hot blanket because he knew I was on the way. He pointed down the dark gully where the van had rolled and wished me luck. His comment was, "Better you than me!" Two ropes were strung full length down the hill, but the patient was well beyond the ends. The hillside had many small patches of snow, was very steep with a few short (two-foot to four-foot) cliffs but did not require technical climbing skills. When we got to the patient, he was conscious but very cold. His injuries were not very serious except for shock. He had been ejected on the downhill side as the van was rolling downhill. He was lucky that he landed at the bottom of a two- to three-foot cliff and the van went above him as it rolled down the hill.

With his shock and the low air temperature, his veins were pretty small. I tried three times to get an IV into his arm and succeeded on the third try. Since it was cold, with ice on the rocks and frost or snow on the rest of the ground, I kept the warm fluid bag hanging around my neck on a string with the tubing down inside my sleeve as I hung on to the side of the litter going down the mountain. I was not able to let loose since there was no spare tubing for me to get away from the litter, so I had to hang on very tightly. When any of us slipped, the belay crew had to hold us and the litter.

Crossing the river at the bottom of the hill was invigorating, to say the least. The river was mostly frozen on top but with running water underneath. We just broke through the ice layer and waded in the two- or three-foot deep cold river water all the way across. The ambulance had been driven back down the road to the highway, and it met us a short distance from the river. I had to take my coat off to get the fluid bottle out through the sleeve while keeping the cannula inserted in the patient's wrist.

The whole operation was over by shortly after midnight, and we went home and warmed up.

– LYNN BUCHANAN

WMRA
8 FEBRUARY 1992

MT. RAINIER NATIONAL PARK. The delegates from the Washington Mountain Rescue Association (WMRA) met in the historic community center at Longmire today. CWMR was represented by Lynn Buchanan, Jim Moberly, Steve Reese, and Joe Roemer. After a welcome by Mount Rainier National Park (MRNP) Ranger John Wilcox, the meeting was chaired by Brad Albro of Bremerton (Olympic MR).

The meeting was a sobering reflection on how policies and personnel change over the years. Only three or four of all the attendees had been in the community center for a major Park-WMRA party some twenty years ago: Wilcox, Buchanan, and maybe Fred Stanley of Ellensburg and Lee Tegner of TMRU. At that time, Mountain Rescue was the only resource available to the Park Service and the Superintendant went out of his way to make Mountain Rescue members welcome at the park. As policies changed, the park started hiring their own "Climbing Rangers" and attempted to handle all their rescues. A major influence was the increased number of people using MRNP and the increasing frequency of injuries and other problems. Helicopter support became easier. A rescue that used to take a couple of days became a matter of hours with a MAST Huey or a Chinook from Ft. Lewis when the weather permitted. With a still greater influx of visitors and a tighter federal budget, the use of volunteers was increasing and there was a bigger place for volunteer Mountain Rescue again.

The minutes of the meeting would be out later, but one of the major discussions was the summer "Standby" at the park. Only a couple of weekends were spoken for at the meeting; the rest will have to be negotiated among the units before summer. This was a real opportunity for CWMR members. The primary reason you would be there was as rescuers, but the rangers in attendance stressed that rescuers were expected to enjoy themselves if there was no mission or until a rescue was called for. A two-person, well-qualified Mountain Rescue team would be at each of the two high camps and could climb the mountain while they were there. This was similar to the WMRA-MAST standby fifteen years before and a great opportunity for long-remembered missions. A benefit of being at the park was the opportunity to climb instead of being cooped up in a hangar.

Three members of CWMR learned about Skate Creek Road this weekend and the back gate to the park when they left the meeting. The road is two lanes and paved instead of the narrow rocky road twenty years before. It is also now closed only when the snow is too deep. The Skate Creek Road is now a great shortcut to Longmire for CWMR.

— Lynn Buchanan

❖ ❖ ❖

HIMALAYAN FOUNDATION
11 NOVEMBER 1996

I was invited to a fundraising dinner in Seattle sponsored by the Himalayan Foundation. It was a bit expensive, but since I had never been to one of their dinners and this one was in Seattle instead of somewhere in California, I decided to go. I drove to Seattle and went to the hotel where I waited for some more climbers to arrive. The second person to arrive was also from Yakima. He used to be a guide on Mt. Rainier. He climbed it about eighty times but got paid for doing so. That was different from those of us who just do it for the enjoyment. His old boss, Lou Whittaker, had made sure all the retired guides got an invitation to spend $200 for dinner! Another old climber, Dee Molenaar, showed up and we took a while to chat. He wrote the definitive book on Mt. Rainier quite a few years ago. He even mentioned me. He commented that he didn't know very many climbers who could afford such an expensive dinner. Most of the folks there were really trekkers and were doctors and attorneys, not real mountain climbers. I did meet a doctor from Yakima who had done a fair amount of climbing locally as well as a trek or two in the Himalaya. (I felt a bit out of place there because I had never been to the Himalayan Mountains.) I sat between two doctors. One was a lady anesthesiologist; the other was a fellow who had been to Nepal several times doing medical work on treks. He was really interested in how city governments work, how they interrelate with county governments, etc. I was not that interested in talking basic civics, but he did have good questions and was an interesting personality, so it was a good evening.

One of the speakers was Ed Hillary, who, with Sherpa Tenzing, was the first to climb Everest. He showed some of the slides he showed last time he was in Seattle just after the 1953 climb. He was somewhat older this time. Next was the mayor of Chamonix, France, Maurice Herzog. He was one of the first team to climb Annapurna, the first climb of an 8,000-meter peak. I went overseas in the Air Force with one of his books that I had had hardbound in Yakima just before I left. It was an early paperbound book of pictures with the text in French. When I had returned to Yakima after my Air Force tour, he was in Yakima to give a talk at the Cascadians, or at the Capitol Theater. Lex invited him to lunch with several of us that were climbers and members of the American Alpine Club, so I got to have him autograph a couple of my books that he had written.

His English at the dinner was a little stilted, but some mayors can give a good speech even in a (to them) foreign language, especially if they are talking about climbing and the history of climbing.

Next, Lou Whittaker introduced his older brother Jim (ten minutes older), and they talked about other mountains. Then a couple of more modern climbers showed slides, and we ended with short speeches by Sherpa Tenzing's two sons and a very short speech by an Ambassador from Nepal.

At 2330, as I was getting my coat from the check lady, a fellow said hello and asked where we had met before. He was Peter Hackett, the doctor who had spent many years in Nepal treating the locals and many of the trekkers that get in trouble with high altitude problems (HACE and HAPE) on the hike in to Mt. Everest. Unfortunately, even with his help, several die there each year. He had been a speaker for a Mountain Rescue seminar on high altitude illnesses many years ago in Rocky Mountain National Park. I was one of the leaders of the Mountain Rescue Association (MRA) at that time and was on the board of the American Alpine Club (AAC); he must have had a really exceptional memory.

The day after the MRA conference that year, a few of us went climbing on the north side of Longs Peak and found a fellow in the Boulderfield staggering around with the classic symptoms of Cerebral Edema. We diagnosed his problem, and then talked him into going down the mountain with us immediately—probably saving his life. (Page 182)

– LYNN BUCHANAN

SEARCH IN A BLIZZARD
22 OCTOBER 2001

Central Washington Mountain Rescue (CWMR) had a call on 22 October 2001 for the rescue of a climber on the south side of Mt. Adams. He was cold, the weather had turned into a blizzard, and he was somewhere near the Lunch Counter. He had a sleeping bag, but he was not sure he could survive the night.

I rode to the mountain in the CWMR truck in mixed rain and snow. With a very strong wind blowing and several inches of snow already on the ground, we made it to the Cold Springs parking lot. Whoever was driving turned the truck downhill and with the front bumper against the log boundary of the lot, shut it off. I suggested we might have trouble backing it up the hill if it snowed and explained that we should turn it around while we were able, but

I was overruled by the driver. There were four of us, Joe Roemer, Joe Buckholtz, my partner, and myself. We decided that we would remain as two teams of two; my partner and I would be one team, the two Joes the other. We gathered our packs, dressed for the rain, and started out up the trail to the Lunch Counter. Our parkas got wet as we started up the trail, but the temperature dropped rather rapidly. Soon we felt that we had parkas made of sheet metal as the water froze on the outside of the cloth. The wind picked up to the point that we started to be very careful as we passed downwind of any trees. We saw none break, but they were bending rather severely in the wind. My partner and I were pretty well matched for speed, so we soon lost sight of Joe and his partner as the blizzard increased in fury. A short time later, Joe reported by radio that he and his partner were going to bivouac until morning. He was having a problem with his leg and the weather was getting too severe for them to continue.

Mt. Adams from the southwest. Crescent Glacier is in the largest snow area just above the center of the picture. The aerial photo was taken in the summer later in the year after the mission. Aerial photo by LKB.

We were still relatively comfortable and with the visibility dropping to thirty to forty feet, I was still able to follow the general route to the flat area below and to the west of Crescent Glacier. At this point, there was a fair amount of new snow accumulating east of the ridge we had to ascend. I was leading, since my partner admitted he did not know the area as well as I did. We went around the south end of that ridge, picking up the old mule trail, even though the rocks were covered with eight to ten inches of snow, and followed it to the top of the ridge. Visibility was dropping to about ten feet in the blowing snow and high wind, but I was confident of our location so we kept climbing. We followed the summertime route most of the time, staying to the east of the low trees and west of the cliff that drops down into the bowl just west of the moraine of Crescent Glacier. We reached a place where the trail went to the west around some outcrops of rock that were only ten to fifteen feet high, so I tried to climb directly up the outcrop rather than trying to face directly into the wind and snowfall where the trail would take us.

The outcrop of rock was covered with ice and as I got partway up, the wind was gusting so hard I was blown off my holds a couple of times. That outcrop is very simple and short when dry, but it was getting pretty difficult in the storm with a half inch of ice coating it. I began to realize that we could get into severe trouble if we continued and either of us got injured, since we had no backup. The base radio was manned by a couple of CWMR members and the SAR deputy, but we had earlier heard them announce that they were going off the air for the night even though they had two teams climbing on the mountain in one of the worst blizzards I had ever tried to climb in.

We had a short conference and decided that if the climber died, that would be one fatality. However, if one of us got injured, there could be three fatalities before morning, particularly with no backup or radio contact. With the rate the snow was piling up on the lee of the ridge, it could become an avalanche area for us to descend into.

We walked back to the south end of the ridge, but our tracks were already filled in by the new, rapidly accumulating snow, making it difficult to determine where we had climbed up. Descending on that south slope would put us into what could become a major avalanche snow slab unless we could determine where we had climbed up, since the slope ran for a long distance down to the south. I figured the east side of the ridge would pose less of a slab danger since we would be roped together and would be descending through the top of any slab that was forming. I did not want any adventure like I had on Baffin Island some years before (Chapter 3).

After checking several places to drop off the short cliff at the top of the ridge, we finally picked a place and started straight down. We reached the bottom of the steep snow slope, turned right, and followed the grade down to the flat area below the moraine. Once on the flat area, we turned east to get to the east side of the flat and go down through the trees rather than taking a chance of being on the snow slope below the south end of the ridge. At some point as we were travelling east, my partner wanted to check our direction. He was a bit confused by the heavy wind and gusts hitting us from several directions. Using his compass was a good idea for a neophyte, so I encouraged him, knowing we were out of any danger area.

We were still roped-up, with about half of a climbing rope and travelling fairly close together to stay in sight of each other. He pointed out which direction his compass said was south and we proceeded to travel that way. I led as he directed me and when he lost sight of my headlamp (about forty feet away), I would stop and he would catch up. Shortly we were working in and out of a rocky gorge that headed west (south by his compass). The visibility was increasing as the trees to the south of us were filtering out some of the blowing snow. I didn't want to keep following that gully; there was a flat area just to our left, so I turned left toward it. At that point there was a group of three trees where I had camped one night many years before. My partner had put his compass away as we turned to the flat area. We then turned about another 120 degrees toward the east from that group of trees to get back on the trail. Shortly after that we could see the road just to our right and there were the tracks that we had made going up, now frozen in the slush.

Crescent Glacier at the top of the picture with its terminal moraine below it. We had been climbing the ridge on the left with the scattered trees on it accessed via the trail in the bottom left of the picture. When returning, we had to descend in the dark shadowed area, then traverse right to the flatter area above the trees in center bottom. When he took his compass out, we were in the area above the tree clump in the bottom center of the photo. North from there is directly up that terminal moraine. Aerial photo by LKB.

After following the road back down to the parking lot, we opened the back of the truck and found it had several packs in it that had not been there when we left. We went around to the doors on the lee side and when we opened them, there were four more Mountain Rescue folks huddled inside trying to stay warm. We got them to move over, and we, cold and wet, climbed in with them. We had a bit of discussion about the weather above and they told us they were waiting for daylight before starting up.

As daylight arrived, several things happened. The fellow "in extremis" radioed that the weather was improving above. He was in his tent that was completely buried, so he had cut the top of the tent and climbed out through the snow that buried it. (We had not been advised of him having a tent.) With good visibility and better weather, he was returning down the normal route and a team from Tacoma (TMRU) was moving to intercept him. The Forest Service had sent a team to cut several large trees that had blown down during the night and were blocking the road. Then we were able to drive back down to the ranger station.

When the driver of the truck got back from his bivvy on the road above, he discovered that the CWMR truck was indeed stuck with its front bumper against the log rail. We had to get another rig with a winch to drag our truck back far enough that it could be turned around and drive out of the parking lot. Shortly after, the TMRU folks intercepted the fellow we were up there to find and we all returned to the Forest Service compound.

Mission over! A success! A couple of months later, my partner got his story published in a magazine. He did not discuss the article with me, so the first I knew about it was when someone told me. He made much of how he, with only four or five trips to Mt. Adams, had taken his compass out, discovered we were travelling north (by his compass, which would have been up the severely steep moraine in the center of the picture on page 194), and he had taken the old fellow (thirty-five or more climbs of Mt.

Adams) back down to safety. It would have been nice to discuss the article with him, but that has not happened. With visibility at ten to twenty feet on the mountain, it is a good thing he knew how to follow a compass so well! (And probably a good thing he had someone to show him where the mule trail was in that field of rocks and snow!)

– LYNN BUCHANAN

THE ICEWORM
EDITION 2007, VOL.1

Aerial photo by Lynn Buchanan.

It has been a few decades since the last edition of *The Iceworm* was published. Maybe we can do it in color and again add to the knowledge of the members of Central Washington Mountain Rescue.

There was a lot of chitchat on the radio during the night of 22 July 2007 about how the Mt. Adams mission was being conducted on Crescent Glacier. Here for everyone's edification is a photo of Crescent, taken from about 8,500 feet on 11 August 2007, a mere couple of weeks later. If you look carefully, you will see a gully with a few patches of snow coming down the mountain in the left lower quarter of the photo. The snow patch (which was frozen pretty hard) that the patient was lowered down that night covered that gully and extended toward the ridge on the left of the photo along the edge of the shadow line.

If you look very carefully, you can see the old mule trail running horizontally along the lower left corner of the photo, then it is visible going up to the top of the ridge where the trees are. The trail travels along the ridge, mostly in the trees. Above the trees it is again visible, winding its way up and then out of the picture on the left side about two thirds of the way to the top of the picture.

The patient was picked up on the viewer's right side of the gully in that big clump of rocks below the little hump, the leftmost hump, of the terminal moraine and well to the viewer's left of the major part of the moraine.

The flat area of snow that was just below the steep snow that night is visible as a flatter area in the alluvial fan below the gully and above the ridge that extends horizontally across the lower left half of the photo. The important thing to keep in mind is that there was several feet of snow covering the whole area across the gully—from the shadowed area on the left (as we see it in the picture) to the foot of the terminal moraine of Crescent Glacier. It all melted out in the couple of weeks following the night mission. Crescent Glacier is the small dead patch of ice on the mountainside above the terminal moraine.

My history of Mt. Adams adventures extends back quite a few years. The first three or four times I climbed Mt. Adams, I parked my two-wheel drive sedan high on the mountain at the last creek crossing. Nature has pretty well eroded the road we used then, but the Forest Service closed it down at the junction with the Around-The-Mountain Trail back in the late 1960s. There were many adventures on Mt. Adams that started at that parking area at the junction; notable among which were the Mt. Adams Mass Climbs, sponsored by the Yakima Chamber of Commerce. There were eleven of these, not all of which reached the summit, but the only ones that did not were stopped because of bad weather.

In those years, we had about 400 climbers each year, many on their first attempt at climbing a snowcapped volcano. We would start up in the dark hours early on a Sunday morning.

This photo was taken 9 September 2007, almost a month after the first photo. You will notice how much more snow is melted, showing more clearly where the actual glacier is located. Aerial photo by LKB.

If any of you attended the Cascadian meeting in 2011, I showed a collection of slides and talked a bit about those adventures. I was up on the mountain a few days (and often a couple of weekends) before the climb to set the route and kick steps to help the inexperienced ones. Central Washington Mountain Rescue members turned out in force to help the chamber put the event on. The Crag Rats of Hood River also sent a contingent of their Mountain Rescue members along to help. We had one Governor of Washington State (Governor Evans, later a United States Senator), a state Attorney General (now United States Senator Slade Gorton), both of whom were real mountain climbers before that time, and several other well-known folks, such as

Ome Daiber as the nominal "Leader" of the climb. My place on the climb itself, however, was to set the pace to keep it steady.

Altogether, I reached the summit of Mt. Adams thirty-five times by four different routes in nine different months of the year. I participated in more than forty-five mountain rescue missions on Mt. Adams, some of which were very interesting, like when the winch broke on a Chinook helicopter at about 10,000 feet elevation and the delay in getting all the rescue party (Seattle MRC) back into the bird resulted in the low fuel warning light illuminating above Toppenish. We made it back to Yakima Training Center with only a few pounds of fuel left in the tanks. There was also the Huey that lost a fuel pump at 10,400 feet on the North Ridge as we were rolling out of the bird. There was the body recovery on the northeast side in the dark when the frozen body in its sled got going faster than the snowmobile towing it below Lyman Glacier and kicked Judy Beehler (a former CWMR member) into the snow from the machine she was riding. There were winter missions and summer missions, foot missions and helicopter missions; there was a search or two conducted in my Cherokee (airplane), one at night by moonlight. I have solo climbed the mountain and led parties of more than 400 up the mountain.

I spent several years on the Membership Committee (a couple as chairman of the committee) of the American Alpine Club (AAC), the national climbing organization. That was when you had to have a significant climbing or exploring record and a recommendation from two current members to get in. I don't think anyone currently in CWMR now belongs to the AAC except me. Lex Maxwell and Davy Mahre were the only others I remember. As Membership Chairman, my committee had six folks from all across the United States, and all would have to agree before we accepted each member—each one of whom had to submit a rather extensive climbing or exploring biography to be accepted. Becoming a member is much easier these days.

In those days, you had to be a mountain climber and had to have led climbing parties to even be considered for rescue membership in CWMR. Now, how many CWMR members have climbed enough to have even seen a real Iceworm?

LYNN BUCHANAN
EDITOR
LYNNBUCHANAN.COM

POSTSCRIPT

The Legends Dinner, Seattle Mountaineers, 9 April 2010:

THE SEATTLE MOUNTAINEERS HAVE a new clubhouse, built in Magnusson Park on Lake Washington. Connie and I were invited to their "Legends" dinner (which was also a major fundraiser for the Mountaineers). The occasion was a celebration of the life of Wolf Bauer (ninety-eight years old). It was also the launching of the book of his life, *Crags, Eddies, & Riprap*, written by Wolf Bauer and Lynn Hyde. Wolf was one of the original founders of Seattle Mountain Rescue, as well as a mountain climber, skier, shoreline engineer, and promoter of the Green River park system.

Jim and Lou Whittaker with Wolf Bauer in the middle

In addition to Wolf's book, three other fellows who were prominent in Seattle climbing and rescue circles were there to sign their books: Jim Whittaker, Lou Whittaker, and Dee Molenaar. Since I was one of those whose rescue biography was in Dee's most recent book, *Mountains Don't Care, But We Do*, I was also asked by a couple of folks to autograph their copies of the book.

Jim and Lou Whittaker with Dee Molenaar, center.
Photos by LKB.

RESIGNATION LETTER:

MR. LYNN K. BUCHANAN
115 West D Street
Yakima, WA 98902
509-248-6841
FAX: 509 248 1457
Email: Lynn@lynnbuchanan.com
Web: www.lynnbuchanan.com
17 May 2010

Ken Irwin
Sheriff, Yakima County
1822 So. 1st St.
Yakima, WA 98901

Dear Ken,

In September 1952, I participated in my first mountaineering body recovery with the Seattle Mountain Rescue Council. The day after that, I climbed the peak again with Ome Daiber to help determine the cause of the accident. As a rather enthusiastic mountaineer, Ome Daiber pointed me to Mountain Rescue as a way to help others in my chosen sport.

It is now May, 2010, after fifty-eight years of active service in Mountain Rescue. I have been fortunate in being able to be in the field on most of the rescues I have participated in, although I did serve as Operations Leader of a mission in Pend Oreille

County for one twenty-four-hour period organizing more than 100 searchers in the field in cold, wet, and snowy conditions. We rotated the OL duties then, so I went back into the field for several days and nights after my duty as OL. I am enclosing a sheet of statistics ("Summary of Mountain Rescue Missions"), so you will get a feel of what has happened in those fifty-eight years. In the eighty-two helicopter missions, there were two where the helicopter had to be hauled back to Ft. Lewis on a truck because of damage incurred as we were flying in. (There have been several hair-raising helo rescue stories.)

There have been a few missions where I provided my aircraft for search or other uses, and I have flown a lot of trips to Ft. Lewis for MAST mission standbys. CWMR felt MAST flights were too dangerous to participate in so two of us from Yakima participated as members of Seattle MRC from 1972 through 1980. When I was on the MAST Committee for Washington State for many years (six as Chairman), I was attending meetings almost monthly, but that mileage and those hours are not listed in the summary.

My enthusiasm for missions has continued, and I have been blessed with a physical ability to go into the field as necessary. I have been the President of Central Washington Mountain Rescue, helped organize the Washington Mountain Rescue Association, and served as the second President of that group. Later, I was the national Mountain Rescue Association President (supported by Seattle MRC, not CWMR).

While working on an obituary for Lex Maxwell for the American Alpine Club, a national organization of mountain climbers (where I served as Membership Chairman and served on the Board of Directors for two years), I Googled "Lex Maxwell" and was reminded again of a rather hairy, but successful, mission back in 1968. It has been an interesting fifty-eight years.

I have assisted the FAA and the USAF on several aircraft accidents and would be happy to help your office on any more of them.

If you check my website (www.lynnbuchanan.com), you will see a few of my past missions and if I am not spending my time in the field, maybe I can put a few more pictures and stories on the site.

I have climbed to mountain summits 197 times, one a first ascent in the Arctic in the winter, another to 18,700 feet in Mexico. I have climbed to the summit of Mt. Adams thirty-five times by several routes. I have responded to missions on that mountain more than forty-five times and spent uncounted days preparing the route and leading the Yakima Mass Climb of Mt. Adams for ten years. I have responded to your office and to other agencies more than 300 times from Alaska to Mexico. I did not keep records for the first sixteen years when Mountain Rescue was the only organized team in Yakima County, so there are many missions not included in the over 300 listed.

After all that history, it has reached the time to resign from Central Washington Mountain Rescue. I will be available to your office if you need me because I do have some expertise that could still be used.

SINCERELY,
LYNN BUCHANAN

Made in the USA
San Bernardino, CA
23 April 2014